To my siblings

Neil and Sandy

heirs with me to this family history

TRIPS TO TOWN

A Great Depression and World War II Era Memoir

Trips to Town: A Great Depression and World War II Era Memoir
Copyright © 2023 Lori Lipsky www.lorilipsky.com
Published by Bamzyl Books LLC
ISBN: 978-1-7365325-5-3 (paperback)
ISBN: 978-1-7365325-6-0 (e-book)

For privacy reasons, some names may have been changed.

Scriptures marked KJV are taken from the KING JAMES VERSION (KJV): KING JAMES VERSION, public domain.

Editing, Interior, and Cover Design by Michelle Rayburn of missionandmedia.com

2023 First Edition

TRIPS TO TOWN
A Great Depression and World War II Era Memoir

As told to

Lori Lipsky

BAMZYL BOOKS

Contents

"Remember me when I am gone away, Gone far away into the silent land."
Christina Rosetti

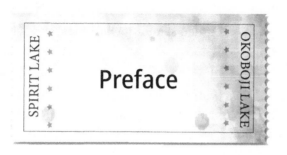

SPIRIT LAKE

OKOBOJI LAKE

Preface

FOR YEARS, I HAD MADE the drive once a week to spend time with my parents. Then in 2019, my mom passed away. I continued my weekly trips, but now Mom, who had been at the center of our conversations, was no longer there.

The idea for this book grew from talks I had with my dad each week. I enjoyed hearing Dad relate true stories from his childhood as much as he liked to tell them. I began to record our conversations and transcribe them after I returned home.

My dad, Neil D. Nelson, grew up in northwestern Iowa during the Great Depression and World War II. He gave me permission to use whatever history he shared with me in any way I chose. As we continued our conversations week after week, the idea to compile the stories of his youth into a book began to form.

Sometimes we conducted informal interviews as we ate lunch together at *The Wedge Inn*, our favorite lunch spot in Janesville, Wisconsin. Occasionally, Dad navigated the country roads to my house, and we'd talk and play games at my dining room table. Most often, though, we sat across from each other at his kitchen table. Before we played pinochle, pitch, Rummikub, SkyJo, or Five Crowns, I'd press the start button on my recorder, slide it toward him, and ask a couple of questions.

Early on, Dad wrote some of his stories down, but when he shared them with me aloud, his reserve fell away, and he was more likely to include an unexpected and oh-so-usable turn of phrase.

This is a collection of stories as told to me by my father, Neil D. Nelson. It's an account of people and events as he remembers them. I've made an effort to verify details when possible. Several names have been changed for privacy reasons.

My dad's long-term memory is remarkable for a man in his nineties. I spent countless hours researching obituaries, newspaper articles, maps, and cemetery records—only to confirm his statements time after time. Through this project, I've been privileged to get to know my dad better. And I've come to know Dad's family, neighbors, and friends in ways I never would have if it weren't for this book. I'm deeply honored to have this opportunity to share their names and stories here.

Lori (Nelson) Lipsky

SPIRIT LAKE

OKOBOJI LAKE

Prologue

MY GRANDPA, DAVID NELSON, IS the reason our family ended up in Spirit Lake, Iowa. In the 1890s, he moved to Spirit Lake from Big Springs, South Dakota, where he had grown up. He found work on a pony ranch on the west side of Big Spirit Lake. There, he met Maude Swailes, an eighteen-year-old girl who lived with her family on a nearby farm.

After marrying, the two moved back to David's roots to begin farming and growing their family in South Dakota. They had four children and buried one of them before they returned to Iowa to purchase and run a farm southwest of Big Spirit Lake. Their children were Marjorie, Neil (my dad, whom I'm named after), and Fern.

Grandpa Dave had plenty of hunting and shooting experience by the time he returned to Spirit Lake. Flocks of whistling swans lived in the area and could be seen in abundance swimming on Big Spirit Lake. People cooked and served the swan as they would a goose until it became illegal to shoot them.

Dave's younger brother Joseph had followed him to Spirit Lake. Joseph's interests were in business, and over the years, he started and ran a number of them. Levi, a younger brother, sold his farm and moved to Spirit Lake to help Joe with his businesses.

When Dave's son, Neil Swailes Nelson (my dad), finished eighth grade, he stopped attending school and began helping on the farm. Soon afterward, with the family farm in the capable hands of his young son, Dave Nelson joined his brother Joe in operating a commercial seining business. I'll discuss seining in more detail in chapter 28.

One day when Dave was away from home, his son borrowed his gun to shoot ducks. Dave owned a double-barreled shotgun called a Damascus barrel. Dave did plenty of shooting to feed his family. To save money, he always loaded his own shells with shot and powder. When young Neil loaded the casings that day, he overfilled them with powder.

> Damascus shotgun barrels were constructed by forging layered strips of steel and iron together. Production of Damascus barrels ceased in the early 1900s.

He snuck up on a big flock of ducks at Jemmerson Slough, the wetland adjacent to their farm. After sneaking as close as he dared, Neil shot.

Instantly, the whole left side of the Damascus barrel blew out and cut almost half of his wrist off.

Neil grabbed his wrist and ran the distance to the house— between a quarter and half a mile. When he showed his wound to his mother, she fainted.

Marjorie, his older sister, took charge and phoned the local doctor. He came to the house and then took Neil to the hospital in Estherville to get him stitched up. Neil never had good circulation in his left hand after that. Years later when he worked on a seining crew in the wintertime, he always had to wear a big mitten for warmth.

Each spring, the three Nelson brothers, Dave, Joe, and Levi, would hire a crew and seine carp from Spirit Lake, East Okoboji, and smaller lakes in the area. Joe secured a buyer for the carp they netted. The brothers gutted the fish and packed them on ice. Then the buyer shipped them to Chicago, Sioux City, Omaha, and other midwestern cities.

In the winter, the brothers started an ice business.

An ice company in Spirit Lake delivered blocks of ice to anyone who owned an icebox. An icebox was a refrigerator cooled by a block of ice rather than electricity. The worker, called an iceman, would take a block of ice out of the truck with large tongs and wash it off with water from the truck. Then he'd carry it and place it in the top compartment of the icebox. The ice company worked out of an old barn by the road between the lake and the town of Spirit Lake.

Dave and Joe were contracted to furnish all the ice for the ice company. Levi helped, plus they hired another man or two. They hooked a big saw to a gasoline engine and cut large squares of ice, which they pulled from the water with huge tongs. Once they pulled the ice blocks up on the frozen surface of the lake, they placed them on wooden slides. They had built the wooden slides to move the blocks to the beach, where they loaded them onto a wagon. They borrowed the horses from Dave's son, Neil, who owned four horses he used on the farm.

Joe and Dave made a deal with two lumber yards to save

all the wood shavings and sawdust from the year before. When they stored blocks of ice in the barn, they covered them with sawdust and shavings to keep them from melting—which explains why the iceman washed off sawdust before placing a block in the icebox of a home, restaurant, or gas station.

Chapter 1

Working on Lorna and Jerry's Farm

THE FOLKS SENT ME TO live with my sister Lorna and her husband, Jerry Kelley, when I was eleven years old. I spent my entire summer working on their farm near Milford, Iowa. Mom and Dad decided it would be a good opportunity for me to learn farming since we had moved off our farmstead when I was seven.

Jerry couldn't afford a hired hand, and with no nearby relative to help him, I was elected. For payment, I received room and board. Lorna and Jerry said they'd give me a dollar to spend if we went to Milford on a Saturday. But that only happened once.

Jerry and Lorna owned twelve cows. I hand-milked four of them twice a day, cleaned out the barn, limed the floor, and sprayed for flies. I also fed and watered about 300 chickens that they raised for eating. This included mixing their feed after using a hammer mill to chop up parts of it. In addition, I fed laying hens and collected eggs each day. I also helped take the sheep out and bring them back to the barn.

I spent much of my time working in Lorna and Jerry's gardens. Like many Iowa farmers, they planted a huge garden in addition to a large potato plot on the other side of their property. I took care of all the weeding and picked strawberries, green beans, and whatever else needed picking.

We cut the alfalfa and put it in the hay mow on a day when it was 110 degrees up there. Jerry had bought a small Model A Farmall tractor. The width of the front wheels could be adjusted to fit between rows of corn to till the soil and shovel out the weeds. I got to use it a lot.

Farming was a hard life, I guess, but we didn't talk about it. We worked from the time the sun went up until after the sun went down. My mother and father were both raised on farms and so was Jerry. People raised on a farm just accepted that sort of lifestyle, I think.

I never saw my parents for that entire summer, even though they were only several miles away. Not even once. That was the toughest thing about that summer for me. I found out I enjoyed farming, though.

....

LORNA AND JERRY'S FIRST SON, Bob, was born that summer. Not long after Bob's birth, Jerry made a trip into Milford to pick up some parts. I was working outside but came into the house when the weather turned bad. Lorna and I heard what sounded like a freight train coming, so we ran into the kitchen, where they had a trap door going down to the cellar. Lorna held Bob while I opened the door in the floor for her. That's when we heard the roar going right over the house. We looked out the window and saw a funnel cloud head down the hill and into the lake. Jerry was driving back from Milford and saw the tornado, so he got out of his car and lay down in the ditch.

The tornado hit farm buildings one mile south of Jerry and Lorna's place and traveled along the road behind the cottages. It raised up as it went over the farmhouse we were in, then came back down to the ground and went into the lake.

One nearby garage held a car at one end and a sleeping housemaid at the other. The twister lifted the garage and carried it away but thankfully left the maid safely in her bed and the car standing in its place when the garage landed.

....

THREE BROTHERS INHERITED A FARM nearby consisting of eighty acres of land that included about a mile of West Lake Okoboji lakefront. At the highway entrance stood two large stone pillars posting the estate name: Egralharve. The three brothers were Egbert, Ralph, and Harvey, but Harvey was the only brother I had ever met. He acted on behalf of the other two owners.

Harvey owned a large two-story cottage on the lake, where his wife, daughter, and grandson stayed all summer. His son-in-law worked as a pilot for United Airlines in Chicago and joined them on some weekends. Harvey owned a new-looking office building in downtown Chicago. I saw a photo of it once.

The brothers sold lots along a half mile of Lake Okoboji. About twelve cottages were built. Most were big two-story homes with large porches on the lakeside and garages behind near the road. The road ran through the farm, then turned ninety degrees south, parallel to the lake.

I worked for Jerry six days a week, but on Sundays, I could do what I wanted. One day, Harvey invited me to go along with them to a dinner engagement on the opposite side of the lake. His grandson didn't know anyone his age in the area and wanted a companion, so I agreed to go. We entered a massive three-story home with huge glass windows overlooking the lake. We were seated at a huge table with many guests. The servers brought out multiple courses of abundant food. My place setting included three knives, three forks, and three spoons. I had no idea which one to use for what food. I was super nervous and had to wait to see what my buddy would use before I dared to pick up any utensil.

....

I DELIVERED MILK FROM THE farm to area cottages and got to know people that way. Since I wasn't paid for working on the farm, I sometimes mowed lawns on Sundays to earn a little cash. I also raked and burned leaves for people.

Joel Herbst, a lawyer from Algona, Iowa, who was about forty years old, owned one of the cottages farther down the lake. He was deeply involved in politics and had worked to get the governor elected. A couple of times while I worked on his big yard by the lake, Joel and Governor Hickenlooper sat on the porch talking. Their wives must have been inside the house—I never saw them.

Hickenlooper was lieutenant governor of Iowa at the time and became governor two years later. He ran for Senate and won that election too. It made me terribly anxious to have the big shots watching over me while I worked.

....

A COUPLE WHO OPERATED A large dairy owned the first big cottage where the road turned. Their two sons were in high school. The family owned a large Chris-Craft boat, a speed boat made from wood with an eight-cylinder motor that enabled it to go thirty-five miles per hour. One boy would run the boat around the lake until it was almost out of gas. They'd stop to fill the boat with gas, and then the other boy would run it around the lake. The family invited me to come over and swim off their dock anytime.

One Sunday, I went over and swam for a couple of hours. West Okoboji isn't an ordinary lake where you can swim out slowly. It drops off fast—here it was ten or twelve feet deep at the end of the dock. That day, one boy stood on the dock while two of us swam way out and back in.

On my turn, I went out and back and then grabbed hold of a round metal pole at the end of the dock to pull myself up onto the deck. Immediately, my hands were on fire.

I was unable to let go of the pole.

The boy on the dock jumped into action and kicked me off with his foot. I woke up when my body hit the bottom of the lake.

It turned out that the electric pole for the light at the end of the dock wasn't grounded. The iron in the water acted as a conductor. The quick thinking of the boy who kicked me from the pole saved my life.

Neil with Bob Kelley, late 1941

Neil, Bob, and Lorna

Chapter 2

On the Farm by
the Slough

I WAS BORN IN 1930, THE year after the Wall Street Crash. Until the age of seven, I lived with my family on a farm in Spirit Lake, Iowa. Despite the Great Depression, many of my favorite memories are from those days. My grandfather, David Nelson, owned the farm, and my parents, Neil and Beulah "Bea" Nelson, worked it.

By the time I came along, my oldest sister Lorna was twelve. Lorna often helped my mother in the kitchen and later in the restaurant. My other two sisters didn't have as many responsibilities. Jean was almost ten years older, and Irene was seven and a half years older than I. My parents named me Neil after my father, but my family called me Bud—Buddy when I was younger.

Times were tough in the 1930s. My folks raised pigs, but no one had money to buy them. One benefit of that difficulty was that we had no shortage of meat like other area families. If we needed meat, my dad butchered one of the pigs. Years later, Jean said that she and Irene were popular with the kids from town because they longed to be invited to our place for a meal. Food was plentiful, and everyone liked my mother's cooking.

After the Crash, the folks not only couldn't sell their pigs, but they weren't able to sell the milk from their dairy cows either. Dad poured oats into two wooden troughs to feed the pigs and mixed in the skimmed milk left after separating the cream. That was their main feed.

Once each year, my parents sold half their corn crop—the only crop they could sell for cash. Grandpa Dave sold the other half to cover the cost of rent since the farm belonged to him. The only other thing my parents could sell was the cream they separated from the milk.

Livestock were important for farming, and the folks raised some crops for feeding them. Dolly and Molly, the pair of horses my dad always used for farming, were fed oats, which Dad stored in the granary. It was the same for the other two backup horses, Daisy and Birdy. Dad didn't feed the animals corn because it was the only crop we could sell for cash.

Dad milked sixteen cows twice a day—they were Guernseys, which are larger than Jerseys but smaller than Holsteins. My dad milked the cows by hand each morning, and in the evening, my mom helped. After the milking, she separated the cream out. Mom and Dad knew each of the cows by name. I was too young to help then, so I never learned the names. Dad fed them timothy or alfalfa—whatever type of hay he grew across the road.

On Saturday afternoons, my folks sold their cream in the town of Spirit Lake. They used the money from the sale to buy gasoline for the car and groceries for the week. In my younger years, they would take eggs to town and sell them too, supplying several customers who bought from them each week.

Life on the farm included pets too. Tricksy and Blacky were our two fox terriers. Blacky was Tricksy's puppy. They slept on the front porch. We also had four cats around the farm. The folks gave the cats milk each day after they milked the cows.

Our biggest pasture was a quarter mile south of the barn. The cows took the lane, guided by a fence on each side of them. The manure pile stood outside the back door of the barn where the cows went in and out. A farm field sprawled on each side of the lane—one east and one west of the fence. Dad planted corn in both. He often planted oats in the big field east of the house, granary, and barn. The field west of it—north and west of our home—grew corn in the years I can remember.

To earn extra money to make up for lacking farm income my dad contracted with Spirit Lake Consolidated School to transport all the children on our road and nearby the road into town. He took out a loan to purchase a black Ford van with windows in the front but not in the back. In the rear of the vehicle, he installed a bench on each side. When I was four, I always wanted to ride with my dad in the front seat, but I only got to go with him a few times.

Years later, I found out Dad would take the kids to school, then stop at the pool hall before heading back home. A game of pool cost about ten cents and gave him a chance to talk with other men since there were none on our farm.

....

MY DAD TURNED UP A lot of rocks every year when he plowed. He and other farmers went out each spring and picked up heavy stones from their fields. Dad used a flat sled with two runners. He heaped the rocks on the sled, and his horses pulled them to the rock pile.

There was a quarter mile between our house and the road, which left space for Dad's pile behind our house. Most farms were closer to the road than ours, so it was common for farmers to unload rocks in the ditch along the road. The large stones provided plenty of places for farmers to hide money and boot-legged whiskey. Most farmers didn't trust banks after the Crash, so they hid their money in the rocks.

Most farmers created their own junkyards too. When a machine broke down, if they didn't pay to have somebody pick it up, they needed to make a place for their old farm equipment.

I rode all over our farm on my broomstick horse and spent a lot of my time playing cowboy. Other kids had a stick with reins and a horse head at top. I always wished I'd had one of those.

In the winter, I often made igloos out in the front yard. I'd build one and hollow it out so I could climb in. I have no idea how I knew about cowboys and igloos before I ever went to school. I didn't listen to stories on the radio until after I started kindergarten, and there were no other kids on the farm to play with.

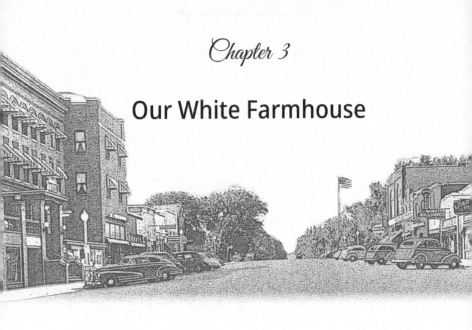

Chapter 3

Our White Farmhouse

WE LIVED IN A SINGLE-STORY, L-shaped house with an attic but no basement or cellar. The house had no back or side door, only a door in front. The front lock had an old skeleton key, but my parents never locked the door. Just about every old house in the area had that sort of lock.

Our home, the corn crib, and the chicken coop were painted white. The barn was newer and painted red. My grandpa Dave and Dad built it in 1924 before I was born. The granary and the hog house had an unpainted, weathered look.

Because the house was set back a fair distance from the road, if anyone drove up to the house, one of the folks would hear them coming and go to the door. We didn't need a doorbell.

Our family shared a telephone line with several neighbors. The phone company assigned a different ring for each home: one ring, one and a half rings, two rings, three rings, etc.

Neighbors could listen in on your conversation if they were nosy enough, and some were.

Our family gathered at a long kitchen table for breakfast and dinner during the school year. The girls and I carried a sack lunch on school days. In the summer, our family ate all three meals together. The kitchen was large and open to what people would now call the living room. Off the back of the kitchen was a small bedroom that my oldest sister Lorna used. She kept the door open in the winter to take advantage of the heat from the stove.

A hallway off the middle of the living room led to the folks' bedroom on the right side. I don't remember ever going into my parents' bedroom. I think they always kept the door shut. On the other side of the hallway was a long bedroom. Jean and Irene shared a double bed to the left, on the far side of the room. The girls had a dresser at their end of the room but no closet. I had a plain double bed to the right as you entered the room and no closet or dresser.

In the winter, Mom stacked covers high on our beds. I'd get dressed in pajamas near the kitchen stove, then run to bed and tuck under the big pile of blankets. In the morning, I'd get up before the girls, run to the kitchen, and get dressed by the stove. Our home wasn't insulated, and ours was the coldest room because it was farthest from the kitchen. In the summer, when I looked out the bedroom window, I could see the front yard, the outhouse, and the trees across the drive leading out to the main road.

I can't remember having a bedtime, but once darkness fell, there wasn't much to do. In the winter, my dad was in the house for meals, and after milking the cows, he'd stay inside at night until bedtime. Most nights, he sat in the living room after supper. There was no television. We didn't play cards or listen to the radio together, and we didn't play games as a family. The kids went to bed before the folks, so I don't know if my parents read at night or not. Sometimes I saw them read the family Bible.

Our family Bible is the only book I remember in the house. We never subscribed to a newspaper because of the cost. We could look through the Montgomery Ward or Sears, Roebuck & Co. catalogs if the folks didn't need them. Old catalogs were put to use in the outhouse in place of toilet paper.

Farming was hard work. In the summer, my dad rose early before everyone else to milk the cows. He worked outside all day except for meals, and he'd often go back outside after supper until ten o'clock at night. He was almost always out of doors it seemed.

Our closest neighbors were the Brumms and the Damms. The Brumm family lived across the road and to the east. Shimmy and Flo Damm were across the road to the west, about equal distance from our mailbox. We couldn't see either home from our house.

Chapter 4

Household Chores

W E USED TWO KEROSENE LAMPS to light the house. Dad took a third large lamp to the barn when heading out to milk early in the morning. Dad hung it high so he could see to do his work.

Mom had a cistern for water. Rainwater off the roof ran down into the tank. She used water from that reservoir for laundry and washing dishes. I think she boiled the cistern water to wash dishes. Our drinking water came from a well located some distance from the front of the house. Behind the barn, Dad had another well with a pump and a tank for the horses and the cattle.

Mom, or whoever she sent out, would carry the water. Lorna was always helping her in the kitchen, so Jean and Irene probably carried the water. I didn't get water often because I was the smallest one, but I did fetch it on occasion.

Lorna was a workhorse around home. She was always helping Mom. I'm not sure how she felt about that, but she later turned out to be a wonderful cook and a good mother.

Once or twice a year, Dad butchered a hog. He'd hang it from the haymow by its legs and cut its throat. Then he lowered it into a large wooden barrel of boiling water so he could skin it. I didn't get to see it being cut up for eating. Mom took the fat from the hog and made the lard she cooked with. She had a huge copper tub with a handle on each end. Each time they butchered a hog, she mixed lard, water, and lye enough to fill the copper tub. The result was the homemade lye soap she used to clean the house and wash clothes.

In addition to the large vegetable and potato gardens the folks planted each year, our family also had an apple orchard. Many farms had a cellar for storing fruits and vegetables, but ours did not. All the area farmers grew carrots. Lots and lots of carrots. Our neighbors had a cellar, and they stored potatoes and carrots down there.

Mom canned almost everything in her pressure cooker. She canned vegetables, tomatoes, applesauce, pork, and chicken.

Sweet corn was the only thing the folks didn't grow in the garden. Before the kernels on the field corn were full, my dad would pick it. Mom cooked the field corn the same as she cooked sweet corn. And we ate it the same.

Our family ate potatoes every day. At least once or twice a day. Mom canned whatever potatoes we didn't eat so they wouldn't rot.

Mom raised chickens, both for eggs and for eating. We ate plenty of chicken. My dad killed and cleaned the chicken, and my mom cut it up and fried it. Mom was pretty good at cutting up chickens. They don't cut them like that anymore at the store. Jean and Irene always fought over the wishbone. They pulled it to see who would get the largest part every time we had chicken.

When Dad would butcher a pig, Mom canned most of that meat. However, we'd have frozen meat from the hog Dad butchered in the fall. No one owned freezers in those days. But the wind was always out of the west, so the folks laid the meat along our cold bedroom wall, and that stockpile supplied the family with food all winter.

A friend of my dad's worked on the Iowa State Commission seining crew. Now and then, he'd give my dad a couple of carp. My mom would fry them. That's the only fish we ever had on the farm. My dad spent all the hours of his days farming—he never went fishing during the years he farmed.

The folks grew or raised all their own food except for sugar, coffee, flour, salt, and a few other items they couldn't make. They never spent money on toothpaste. We used baking soda or salt. We'd put salt or soda in the palm of our hand and dip our toothbrush in it before brushing. In later years they bought toothpaste, but money was scarce when we were on the farm.

Mom's washing machine was an old-fashioned wringer with a crank that needed to be turned to operate it. Dad had to start the gasoline engine to run the agitator before she could use it. The washing machine was kept on the front porch—the same one where the two dogs slept.

We had a kerosene stove in our living room that provided the heat for the entire house. Dad poured the kerosene into a tank on the back of the unit. The only other heat source on cold days was the kitchen stove.

The cast iron stove in the kitchen took chopped wood for fuel. It had four or more cast iron parts that could be removed with a metal handle when they were either hot or cold. The stove had a chimney with a damper on the pipe going out through the roof. The lower portion was a large oven, which Mom used to bake almost every day of the year.

My sisters Jean and Irene spent a lot of time playing together, but they didn't include me in their play. I'm not sure why. I once heard Jean tell Irene that farm boys always had all the advantages, and girls usually had none. I think she meant that the oldest boy would often inherit the family farm. It seemed to me they'd been happy having three girls in the family and had no interest in having a brother.

(from left) Jean, Lorna, and Irene before Neil came along

When we were older, Jean told me that Dad would send her and Irene down to the pasture to bring up the cows, and more than once, they became distracted in their play and completely forgot about bringing up the cows. She also told me that Dad used to raise sheep and shear them. He used that money to pay off the insurance, but he got tired of working with sheep and sold them off.

He must have sold them when I was three or four because my earliest memory is of two lambs my mom kept in a box in the kitchen to keep them warm. My mother nursed the two lambs using a baby bottle with a nipple. When I was older, I realized that the sheep's mother must have died, and Mom had fed the lambs to keep them alive. I thought the little lambs were the sweetest things in the world.

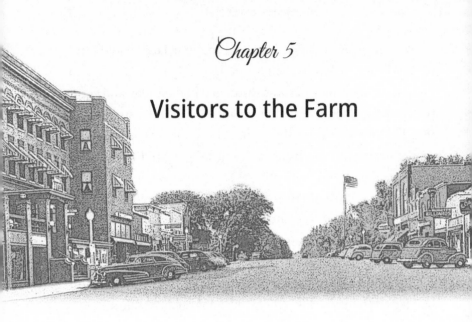

Chapter 5

Visitors to the Farm

DURING THE DEPRESSION YEARS, PEOPLE worked hard just to keep their families fed and sheltered. As far as I know, farming families around Spirit Lake didn't host a lot of company. Most saved their socializing for trips into town on Saturday and maybe a dance on Saturday night.

Visitors were infrequent on our farm. One time a younger couple stopped by. I didn't recognize them, but as I listened, I learned the two had worked for my folks when my mother became ill after I was born. I learned a lot about my early months that day.

Around the time I was born, the folks moved from the Sherk's farm to Grandpa Dave's farm. After my mother delivered me, she "had trouble with her nerves," as some said, and suffered a breakdown. Maybe moving to a different farm and delivering me was more than she could handle. I learned that her doctor had recommended rest and told her she should drink a small glass of beer each day.

Dad had to obtain a permit to buy a small still to make beer. Liquor and beer were both illegal in Iowa. I don't know where he got the ingredients or where he kept the still. I never saw it and never asked. At the time, pale was available—a beer without alcohol in it. Maybe he bought pale and made a little alcohol to mix with it.

Following my birth, the folks sent my sister Jean to live with John Baker and his family. John was my mom's brother. Jean said they treated her well, and she enjoyed her time there. My parents sent Irene to stay with Kate Browning and her family. Kate was my mom's sister. Irene said she was miserable while she lived there. Cousin Neola was mean to her. Neola was always nice to the rest of us, so we never knew what to make of that.

....

MOM'S SISTER MILDRED DROLL AND her whole family came to visit us on the farm once. My mother told me I was too young to play with the boys, Ray Jr. and Johnny, so I kept my distance. I heard stories later of how the two destroyed things while playing unsupervised in the granary. Mildred's girls Leah Jane, Peggy, Evelyn, and Molly, stayed in the house and played with my sisters. Nancy Ann, the youngest, stayed with her mother.

Sometimes we were the ones to do the visiting. We went to the Droll family once. They lived in a house in the town of Dickens, just east of Spencer. Mildred's husband, Ray, sold electric generators to farms. They had a small windmill to run the generators when the wind was blowing. The generators ran with a gasoline motor when there was no wind. Later, Ray got a job as an electrician in a factory in St. Louis, so the family moved there.

Another man dropped by our farm on occasion. The Spirit Lake man sold Watkins products—nutmeg, ginger, other spices, and a variety of kitchen products—to farm families in the area. The guy was about my brother-in-law Jerry Kelley's age. Jerry used to meet him for coffee and conversation.

The man experienced such success selling to area farmers that he was able to open a Pontiac garage in town. Later, he built a place on the edge of town not far from the cemetery. His business was a large gas station where people could also stop for coffee or meals. Eventually, that burned down.

Some visitors had other reasons to stop by. While we lived on the farm, a suitor came to call on Jean—a classmate of hers named Wesley. He played saxophone in the school band. The saxophone happened to be my favorite instrument. Wesley was a big guy and not very athletic. Jean didn't like him very much, but he invited her to the school dance, and she was glad to be able to go.

Except for Jerry, Wesley was the only boy who came calling at the farm. Jean and Irene moved out to California later, and each met her husband there.

One visitor came every day: the mailman. Our mailbox was out by the road, and Dad brought the letters in after he drove us home from school. Often when I sat at the table to listen to the radio after school, there would be ads lying on the table. After saving a number of proof-of-purchase labels from a product, kids could send them in along with money and receive a prize. We used to receive a lot of those types of ads. I would have loved to send in for a prize, but I never had any money.

Chapter 6

Sibling Struggles

AROUND THE TIME I WAS four and five years old, the folks were often away from the house on Saturday nights when they'd go out dancing with another couple. At the same time, my oldest sister Lorna went on dates with Jerry, her husband-to-be. That left me at home to suffer with my older sisters Jean and Irene.

One of the small rooms in our farmhouse had space for a feather mattress and not much else. The girls would lock me in the room, then stand on the other side of the door and tell me all the bad things that were going to happen to me. I suppose they thought it was funny.

Jean enjoyed telling me scary stories about the boogeyman who stayed down in our barn. She told me the boogeyman had big plans to come and get me. Sometimes, one of the girls would hold a pillow over my face, and I would think I was going to die.

Dad got the girls a large brown and white horse. They called the good-looking horse their pony. In the winter, Pony would pull them on a sled, and in the summer, he pulled them around in a buggy.

Pony preferred to live in the barn. He seemed determined to head there whenever possible. Dad was the only one who could keep Pony from going down to the barn.

Sometimes when Dad was away from home, the girls opened the bottom half of the door to the barn and shut the top half. They'd fetch me and help me up on the horse. Pony always proceeded right to the barn, lowering his head to get through the doorway. My body hit against the top door, and I tumbled to the ground behind the horse. My sisters thought it was funny, but they almost killed me. Imagine being four years old, running into the side of a barn, and flying off a horse onto the cement slab at the doorway. This happened more than once, but I never told the folks any of these things.

When I was four and the girls were all in school, I saw a lot of farm happenings, and I really enjoyed that. I learned a lot by watching. I even watched them butcher pigs.

The girls weren't home when Pony died, but I remember it well. Horsehide blankets were highly desirable at the time, especially for lap blankets in a carriage. My parents called Leo Kinniston to come out to the farm that day. When he hung up the girls' horse and skinned it, I watched him do it. My folks paid him for his work. I think the rendering works took the rest. The folks either sold the blanket or gave it away as a gift, but I never saw it around the house. I'm sure they didn't want the girls to know what happened or to see the blanket made from their Pony.

As I grew up, my relationship with Jean and Irene changed. The girls treated me well and were kind. But when we were young, it was a different story.

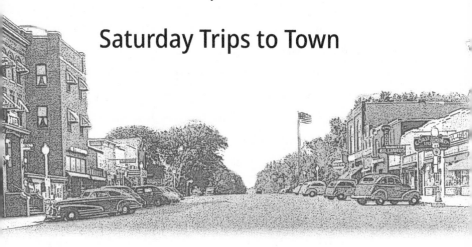

Chapter 7

Saturday Trips to Town

S ATURDAY WAS THE DAY FARM families drove to town to buy supplies. Dad had a mid-sized four-door Ford he'd purchased from the Ford dealer in town. He kept the car in our garage, down the hill from our farmhouse. Every Saturday afternoon, our family would drive into the town of Spirit Lake together.

Dad would pull the car out of our garage, drive up the hill, and park right in front of the house. After a short time, he'd honk the horn. He never considered that besides getting herself ready, my mom had to make sure three kids were ready to go too.

I was blessed with unruly cowlicks, one on each side of the back of my head. Jean was the only one who could do anything with them, so she was put in charge of my hair. She'd wet them down with a concoction and make me look presentable.

In those days, families only had one car, and women didn't usually drive, especially when the couple rode together. Mom and Dad always sat in the front. I sat in the back seat between Jean and Irene. Lorna didn't go to town with us. By the time I was four, Lorna was sixteen and dating Jerry Kelley, so she'd go with him instead.

As we drove toward town, I enjoyed hearing Jean and Irene sing whatever songs were popular at the time. Dad always stopped at the filling station at the bottom of the main business street. The station employee would hand-pump five gallons of gas into the container connected to the upper portion of the gas pump. It showed a mark for each gallon. Once the container was full, he placed the end of the hose into the tank opening and let the five gallons run in. Gravity did the work of getting the gasoline into the vehicle. Five gallons of gas cost one dollar.

If the car needed an oil change, Dad would drive over a pit at the service station. The worker went down the steps into the pit and drained the old oil. He'd come back up and dispense the right number of quarts into a large metal can with a spout. Then he poured that amount into the engine.

My folks sold their cream to a store at the bottom of the hill across the street from the gas station. This same store also sold garden seeds by the pound, or whatever portion of a pound customers wanted. My parents always bought their seeds there.

After selling the cream, Dad would walk up near the pool hall and talk to other farmers. Mom stood on a street corner near the middle of town and visited with other farm women. My folks eventually bought groceries with the money they earned from the sale of their cream.

Until I was old enough to go to the movies, I needed to stay by one of the folks whenever we went to town. I never knew what Jean and Irene were doing, but Jean told me many years later that they would always buy a Clark candy bar and save the wrappers to get a prize. And once in a while, Dad would buy them a chocolate pop.

Chapter 8

Downtown Spirit Lake

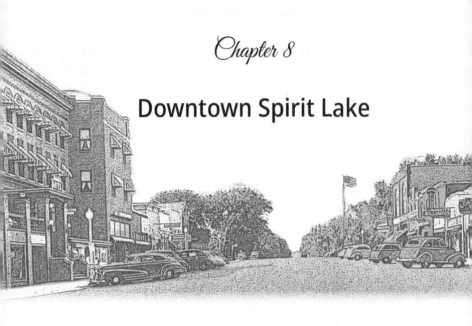

S PIRIT LAKE WAS TWO TOWNS in one. From September through May it seemed like an average Iowa farm town. Our main street was lined with cement sidewalks on both sides. Store owners did their best to keep the area in front of their shops looking clean and inviting. I knew the names of all the business owners. I think everyone did.

Anyone walking down Hill Avenue, the main business street, would not see many cars parked in front of shops. That all changed each year when the summer season started.

The summer months brought lake tourists to the area. When the tourists opened their lake cottages for the season, the boat liveries opened up for business as did the seasonal lakeside shops and food establishments.

Each summer, Hill Avenue transformed from quiet to bustling. Many more cars could be seen parked along the street as vacationers came to town to pick up groceries and other supplies. The drycleaner who may have seen only several customers each day during the school year now had two truck drivers running around from dawn to dusk picking up and dropping off orders.

The water tower rose above every other structure in town. The courthouse, a large two-story brick building, stood on the corner where Highway 9 intersected with Hill Avenue.

South of the courthouse, the Spirit Lake Consolidated School, another two-story brick building, covered an entire block. Like the courthouse, the school was on the west side of the street. The Antlers Hotel, a multi-story brick building, was situated in the center of town. Just inside the front door was the telegraph office, run by Elnora Nelson, Joseph Nelson's wife. Joe was my Grandpa Dave's brother. After I married, my wife DorEtta worked as a waitress in the Antlers Hotel's sizable dining room while I was stationed at Army camp in the state of Washington.

The Spirit Lake Police Station stood across Hill Avenue from the courthouse. To the south of the police station was the library, and south of that, the bowling alley.

Spirit Lake had three hardware stores. On the west side of the street was the Coast to Coast. Across the street stood the privately owned one. Down at the bottom of Hill Street was the Gambles store. One young guy ran Gambles on his own— he didn't have as much business as the other two stores. I went to him if I had trouble with my bike chain or needed help with my bike. He always helped me fix it and only charged for parts.

The Arps owned the nicest grocery store in town. It was up the corner on Hill Street across from the theater. Maybe they had a little better quality, but the prices were higher. My folks shopped at the A & P on the other side of town, where it wasn't quite as expensive.

THE SPIRIT LAKE WATER TOWER was located southeast of the library. My friends Harry Smith, David Dean, and Don Ahrens once made plans to climb the water tower when we were in high school. They talked me into joining them. I don't care for heights, but since they were going, I went along.

We climbed an angled sort of ladder. Toward the top of the tower, a large ring circled the perimeter. The ring was in place for workers to hold on to if they needed support. To get to the top, we had to climb around the ring—that was the hardest part of the adventure. Especially on the way down.

That part wasn't easy at all. We needed to climb back down over the ring to get our feet on the crooked ladder and make it down to the ground again.

It wasn't the best day of my life. Far from it. I'm pretty sure I was the only one of us who was scared to death. But we made it up and down the tower. No one else ever knew about it. We didn't want to get in trouble with the police, so we didn't share the secret. I never told people much about anything anyway.

Hill Avenue, Spirit Lake, Iowa

Chapter 9

My Cousin Jack

AS I GREW OLDER, WHEN my folks would go to town on Saturday afternoons, I'd sometimes get to see a matinee movie at the Spirit Lake theater. On Saturdays, many kids from town would go to the movies. They'd sit down in the first two or three rows and yell and scream as they watched. Oftentimes, the movie was a Western.

One Saturday, when we were about five or six, my cousin Jack (we called him Jackie when he was young) came into town with my family. My folks went shopping and allowed us to see a movie. We didn't go down in front. We didn't know those kids, so we sat in the middle of the theater. Near the very beginning of the movie, an actor came on the screen and aimed his gun right at us. Jack got up and ran out of the theater. No matter what I said, I couldn't talk him into going back inside with me. He thought he was going to get shot.

In the 1930s and 40s, motion picture companies always played a special before the featured movie. Sometimes they showed cartoon shorts or a major world news announcement. My favorite pre-movie attractions were the short *Lone Ranger* episodes.

In the first week of the series, they showed the Lone Ranger starting out his career with the Texas Rangers. The bad guys shot and killed all the Texas Rangers except the one remaining ranger—the Lone Ranger. Each Saturday, the theater would reveal a new episode. Usually, a bad guy would commit a crime, such as robbing a stagecoach. The Lone Ranger would go after him, riding a white stallion named Silver. Tonto was his sidekick. Tonto called the Lone Ranger *Ke-mo Sah-bee*, which meant trusted friend. When the Lone Ranger galloped off at the end of each short episode, a voice would say, "Who was that masked man anyway?"

My cousin Jack and I started kindergarten together. A few times a year, he came and stayed overnight with us, or I'd stay with him. If I went to his place, his family taught me how to play Old Maid and other card games. I always enjoyed it. When Jack came to the farm, he'd be okay until bedtime. We'd be about ready to go to bed, and he'd get homesick. Usually, the folks would have to take him home.

We didn't get together very often. But even when they moved over by Superior—the other side of Spirit Lake—I went to their place and stayed a couple of times. One day when we were in sixth grade, I even went to class with Jack. I met his classmates. I don't know why I didn't have to go to my own school that day.

Jack's father, John Baker, was my mother's older brother. Uncle John lost his farm when we were in fourth grade—the depression crushed many farmers—so their family lived in town for about a year. Then my uncle Wils (John's brother) found a farm about a half mile down the road from his, on the other side. Uncle John rented that farm or took it on shares, and they lived there for a long while.

Uncle John was diagnosed with cancer of the stomach when he was sixty-five. He traveled to Iowa City for all his radiation treatments. They finally killed the cancer, and he lived to be ninety-six years old.

When my cousin's folks retired, they bought a small house in Spirit Lake. Jean, Irene, and I stopped by the house in Spirit Lake when Uncle John was in his nineties. He was out behind the house working on his little garden back there. He had a hard time walking, but there was not one single weed in his garden. I was impressed by that. Our Aunt Maude was doing pretty well too. She ended up living to be 101.

When my wife and I were in our late seventies, we finally met up with my cousin Jack (he now goes by John) and his wife. We'd heard from relatives that they lived an hour away from us. For ten or twenty years, we sometimes said that we should get together, but before we reached out, Jack got in touch with us. The four of us met for lunch at a local restaurant. After lunch, we invited them over for dessert and games. After that day, until my wife passed away, we got together every few months for lunch at the Cracker Barrel restaurant, followed by games of dominoes and pinochle at our home.

Chapter 10

Cousin Novella

MY COUSIN NOVELLA LUCILLE (PARR) Arkfield was a beauty queen. I've always thought she was the nicest looking of all the girls on the Baker side—my mother's side—of the family. When we were much older, my sister Jean made the same comment.

Novella dated the band leader Lawrence Welk for a while, but her parents discouraged the relationship because Lawrence Welk traveled so often with his band. They didn't think she should marry a man who traveled for a living.

Novella's mother, Margaret, was my mom's older sister. After having Novella, Margaret got a divorce. She then married a man named Albert Grady. Together, they had four boys. When Albert Grady died, Margaret remarried her first husband, Novella's dad, and they had another girl together.

My aunt Margaret died at the young age of thirty-four after delivering her seventh child. One of her sons was Joe, a big, husky guy who was especially close with my folks. He often stopped over to spend time with our family.

Novella married Ben Arkfield from Pipestone, Minnesota. I don't know what Ben did for a living, but they moved around a lot. The young couple lived in Spencer, Iowa, for a while, then moved to Pipestone for a couple of years. California was next, and afterward, Webster, South Dakota, where they were in the cafe business.

Novella became ill, so they returned to Spirit Lake to be near family. Novella stayed at the Mayo Hospital in Rochester, Minnesota, for nine months. When it was no longer affordable to have her lie in a hospital, the young couple stayed with our widowed grandmother, Minnie Baker. Later, they moved in with Neola and Hans. Neola was the daughter of one of my mother's older sisters. Neola and Hans lived near us when we were on the farm—right next door to the Brumm family.

I couldn't pronounce Novella's name when I was young. It sounded as if I was saying "vanilla," and everyone always laughed.

When I was six or seven years old, I went with my mother to visit Novella at Neola's place. We didn't see her husband, Ben—he was running errands at the time.

Novella lay in bed, her stomach badly swollen because of ovarian cancer. She was a kind and lovely person. And she was such a beauty before the cancer.

Novella died from ovarian cancer when she was just twenty-eight years old.

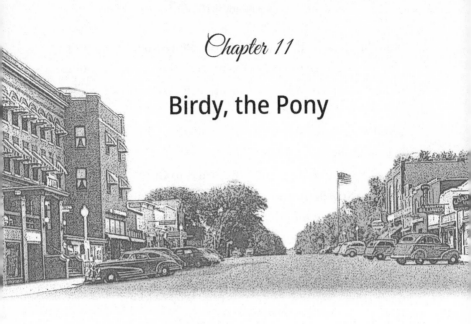

Chapter 11

Birdy, the Pony

M Y DAD BROUGHT A SHETLAND pony home for me one day. That was the biggest and best surprise of my life. A man had offered to sell and deliver her for fifteen dollars. The pony's neck had a big kink about halfway up the mane, having been broken when a mule bit her. Dad called my pony Birdy. It must have been his favorite name. He had a horse named Birdy, plus Jean and Irene's horse "Pony," that died, was named Birdy by Dad too.

When the man delivered the pony, Dad and I went out by the fence in front of the hog house. We put the bridle bit in her mouth, and I scrambled up on her back with the reins in my hand.

Dad went behind the pony and pulled its tail.

The pony bucked, and I flew over the barbed wire fence into the hogs' yard, where it was all muddy. I'm not sure why my dad did that. Maybe he wanted to see if I could hold on, or maybe he thought it would be funny. I was too happy with the pony to worry about it. I got washed up and all but forgot about it.

The pony came with a bridle and nothing else. We never owned a saddle, but I didn't need one. I knew the Indians guided their ponies by using pressure with their knees so their hands would be free to shoot bison with a bow and arrow. I taught Birdy to go left with pressure from my left knee and right with pressure from my right knee. Eventually, I got her to stand up on her hind legs while I was on her back, holding the reins. I'd even take her out in the lake, and she'd swim all over with me on her back. She wasn't the least bit afraid of the water.

Two neighbor kids who lived about a mile away would bring their Shetland pony to our place and want to race. These kids had a relative who visited their family every summer. He worked as a lion tamer. They told me a lot of stories about their relative, and I decided it would be great to be a lion tamer one day.

The neighbor kids and I would race from the Brumms' mailbox to ours. Their pony was two or three years old, and my pony was just plain old. After a couple of races, I gave up on it. Birdy may have been old, but she was the most intelligent animal I was ever around. She could learn almost anything.

We moved off the farm when I was seven. Because we no longer had land or a barn for my pony, a farmer over by the lake boarded her for me for five dollars a month. After a few months, Dad sold the pony because we couldn't afford the board.

Chapter 12

Mom's Cooking

WHEN MY MOM WAS A senior at Spirit Lake High School, she quit school. Three of her brothers—Bert, John, and Wils—were farming together, and they asked her to cook and keep house for them. This was when all of them were still single and a few years before my folks were married.

My mom was a terrific cook. During the years we lived on the farm, Mom cooked breakfast, lunch, and dinner for our entire family every day, seven days a week. Many moms did the same thing. There were no drive-through restaurants at the time, and we probably couldn't have afforded that anyway.

Mom included potatoes with at least one meal every day. Often, two meals a day. Like our family, many area farmers kept a potato garden as well as a regular garden. Potatoes were inexpensive and filling.

My mom raised her own chickens, so we ate poultry a lot. Once in a while, she would buy a tamed rabbit and we'd have that, but I refused to eat rabbit. So Mom would give me something else to eat. When we were seining, my dad sometimes brought home one or two snapping turtles for dinner. Mom fried the turtle the same as she fried chicken, but I wouldn't eat turtle either. The folks also enjoyed eating oysters. I would eat the white oyster soup broth, but I wouldn't eat any oysters. Now and then, Mom made chicken chow mein too, but, you guessed it, I wouldn't eat that either.

On a rare occasion, Mom got a break from cooking. Once, when I was about five years old, my folks were leaving in the car. To where I didn't know. They told me to get in and took me along. I didn't know where Jean and Irene were at the time, and I didn't ask. It was summertime, and we drove to the north end of Lake Okoboji to a building that housed a boat livery on one side and a restaurant on the other. The husband ran the boat livery, and his wife ran the little restaurant.

I had a bacon sandwich. I don't know if I chose it or if one of my folks ordered it for me, but it was about the best thing I had ever eaten in my life! To this day, over eighty years later, I love bacon sandwiches.

That's the only time I can remember in my entire childhood that the folks went out to a restaurant where my mother wasn't the cook. I think they probably went out to eat with friends on a Saturday night a few times. But they never once took my sisters and me to a restaurant. I don't remember ever going out to eat with them another time in my whole life. When I was twenty-two or twenty-three years old, I still lived with them during the summers—up until the day I got married—and we never went out to eat to give my mom a break from making meals.

Chapter 13

Dad's Ditties

FRAMED PHOTOS OF MY PARENTS hang on the wall in my bedroom. In the photo of Dad, he wears a sober face, but I don't remember ever seeing him look like that while I was growing up.

Dad was smiling and fun-loving. I never saw him have a sour look on his face in my life. My mom was a worry wart. She struggled with anxiety, but as her opposite, Dad was blessed with a cheerful personality.

When my dad was around others, he liked to tell jokes. While he worked outside on the farm, he sang ditties and folk songs. He was always singing a tune. I spent a lot of time outside with him and always enjoyed his songs.

He would sing "A Hunting We Will Go," "Billy Boy," and "The Old Grey Mare." Other favorites were "Pop! Goes the Weasel," "She'll Be Comin' Round the Mountain," and "I've Been Working on the Railroad."

When Jean and I were well-past retirement, she told me I missed out on a lot of the good stuff with Dad. Maybe things changed with him because the challenges of the Great Depression affected his ability to make a living from the farm. Money became tight. He worked incredibly hard. However, not being able to sell the hogs and most crops he grew brought stresses he hadn't known earlier when Jean and Irene were younger—before the Crash of 1929.

Jean said Dad used to spend a lot of time with the girls. They had all sorts of fun with him. In addition to all the fun Dad created with their horse, Pony, he often played games with them.

At night he would go in and tell them a story. He'd never told bedtime stories to me. I only heard one, and I've never forgotten it.

I snuck out of bed once in my young days, back when the girls used to sleep near the kitchen.

I heard Dad say to them, "The night was dark and dreary, and the sky was full of blood, and down along the roadside lay a wounded . . . TATER BUG!"

....

ONE DAY, MY DAD SAID, "Come here, Bud. I want to show you something."

We walked together out near the place where he had started the wagon up the hill. He'd brought his axe along, and we stopped by a small tree. Dad took the axe and swung it as hard as he could at the sapling.

The axe just bounced back.

"Son, that is an ironwood tree," Dad said.

....

DAD OWNED AN AMAZING PAIR of Belgian horses. Dolly and Molly were exactly the same size and pulled together beautifully as one. When Dad picked the corn at harvesttime, they walked alongside him at just the right pace across the field. Dad picked the corn by hand and tossed it into the wagon. Dolly and Molly pulled forward without Dad needing to say a word to them.

One year, a horse team pulling contest was going to be held nearby. Dad must have been hoping to enter the contest.

He hitched Dolly and Molly to our big wagon, led them to the gravel pit, and filled the wagon with gravel. He brought it up by the front of the house on the gravel road. A big hill stretched from the front of the house to the rear of the house. Dad chained the four wheels, making them unable to turn. Dolly and Molly pulled the wagon load up the hill with all four wheels chained.

Plenty of men participated in pulling contests with their horses. Contestants needed to pay a fee to enter, but with money being tight in our family, Dad must have struggled over whether to take the risk and pay the entrance fee. In the end, rather than risk losing the money, he chose not to participate. I know he would have loved to, though.

Chapter 14

The Weather of 1936

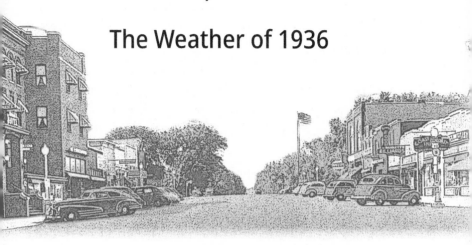

T HE SUMMER AND WINTER OF 1936 were the worst weather-related seasons of my lifetime.

The July 1936 Heat Wave was the warmest of the century on record. Right in the middle of the Great Depression, the United States endured a string of record-setting days of heat. Some of those records still stand. Crops were destroyed by sweltering temperatures and lack of rain. Our house had no air conditioning, and we never owned a fan while we lived on the farm.

The 1936 North American cold wave was just as bad. Temperatures dropped well below zero in January and stayed there for over a month. Our family was snowed in for three or four weeks that winter. I spent much of my time in our front yard building igloos, forming blocks of snow and stacking them to create a dome and leaving an open doorway so I could climb in and out.

Our family was running out of basic necessities. The folks didn't own a sleigh, so Dad placed skis on our heavy farm wagon in place of the four wheels. He attempted to cut across the field to the road. The horses walked across the ice-crusted snow, but after several steps, they'd break through. The wagon was just too heavy. My dad finally gave up. He struggled to turn the horses and their load around and get them back to the barn.

The next day, Dad bundled up and walked south about a mile over our farmland and across the frozen slough adjacent to our property. When he reached the railroad tracks, he found a two-man hand car on the tracks, and he used it to get into town. The hand car handles needed to be pushed up and down to move it forward.

He bought flour, sugar, coffee, and the other items we needed. He carried them to the railroad car and returned home the same way he had come.

We were snowed in fairly often when we lived on the farm, but usually not for long. The winter of 1936 is the one time I remember that we were secluded long enough to run out of food and essentials.

Spirit Lake, Iowa, 1936 [1]

---

1. "FI0002907," Spirit Lake, IA, 1936, Donated by Christina Suarez / Forte-
pan Iowa. CC-BY-SA, https://fortepan.us/photo/269/FI0002907/.

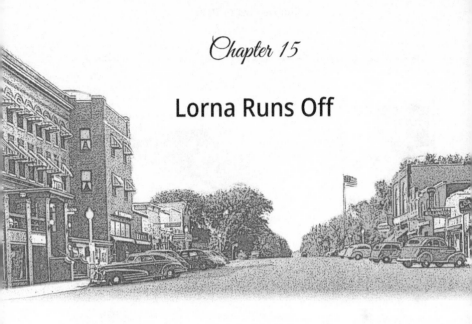

Chapter 15

Lorna Runs Off

MY OLDEST SISTER, LORNA, GRADUATED from high school in June of 1936. At the time, she and Jerry Kelley had been dating for a couple of years. Jerry was three years older than Lorna. He worked at a hardware store in Milford, Iowa.

One night, Lorna went on a date with him. She didn't come home that evening, and she didn't phone. The folks got super worried. Our entire family piled in the car and drove all over, looking for them. Eventually, Lorna called and told us that she and Jerry had eloped. They'd driven to Jackson, Minnesota, and said their vows in front of a justice of the peace. I never did hear all the details.

Lorna was eighteen years old at the time. Most women in those days married around the age of eighteen or nineteen. Sometimes, a woman married at twenty-three or twenty-four, but that wasn't common. These days, it's not unusual for women to marry in their thirties, but expectations were different in the 1930s. Twenty-three was considered old back then.

Not long after their marriage, Jerry got a job running the water plant in Milford. The newlyweds lived in an upstairs apartment on one of Milford's main streets. Their place was over a shop on the east side of the street, and they could park their car in the alley behind the store. Lorna and Jerry had their own steps in the back that led to their apartment. The unit included a small outside balcony too.

I visited them for a weekend once while they lived in Milford. Jerry knew a man who worked at the meat market, so we stopped by, and he showed us how he made wieners and sausages.

Jerry had a younger brother, Ron. When the two were growing up, their folks struggled to make a living farming. Their family lived in Ruthven, which lies between Spencer and Emmetsburg. When Jerry's parents realized they could no longer earn enough money to care for their family, they'd sent Jerry to live with an aunt. He ended up staying with his aunt for a long time, and she became like a mother to him.

Chapter 16

The Chicken Thief

THE FOLKS DISCOVERED THAT SOMETHING or someone was stealing their chickens. The thefts happened after our family left for town on Saturday afternoons. Whoever it was would wait for us to ride away together. We wondered if we were being watched, but we weren't sure. Either way, the thief used that opportunity to steal our chickens.

Dad heard about a big dog that was available. A man named Jim owned a beer distribution business and a warehouse in Spirit Lake. Jim lived with his wife and son in a home they owned on East Okoboji Lake, about halfway to Orleans.

They chained their dog in their front yard. When their young son came home from school each day, he threw rocks at the dog before going inside. The dog became too mean to keep, so Jim gave the dog to Dad.

My dad bought a muzzle and brought the dog home. Pal was a large black dog, bigger than a German Shepherd. Dad chained Pal to a tree in our front yard so all of us could walk outside without Pal hurting us. After three or four weeks, Pal calmed down. I'm sure he realized that no one would throw rocks at him anymore. He was safe for us to be around, so my dad turned him loose on the farm. After that, no more chickens ever disappeared on Saturdays when we went to town.

One day, we were looking across the oat field east of the house, out toward the main road. A big German Shepherd came running toward us barking and snarling. Pal took off at full speed to meet the intruder. Pal chased the dog out through the fence and back to the main road. We never found out where the dog came from.

The next year, when we moved off the farm, we could only keep one dog. The folks gave Blackie and Pal away but kept Tricksy. Tricksy was an old dog, about the same age as my sister Lorna. I never saw Blackie or Pal again.

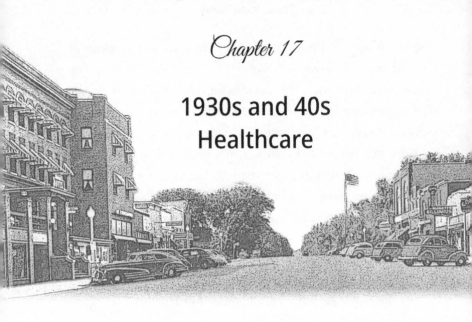

Chapter 17

1930s and 40s
Healthcare

WHEN I WAS GROWING UP, we never took medication. I never once took an aspirin or an antacid. Our family never had pills of any kind in the house. With money tight, it meant they avoided calling the doctor for anything. Doctors often drove to patients' homes on house calls, but I don't remember ever having a doctor come to our house.

Schools required students to have an exam and shots before entering kindergarten. My mother drove me to the doctor's office in town for the shots. Not many moms drove, but mine did.

After the appointment, the doctor told my mom that Tommy Carver and I were the healthiest kids entering kindergarten. Of course, this was long before the days of medical privacy laws.

Mom often yelled at Irene and Jean about going barefoot out in the farmyard, but they did it all the time anyway. They were always playing outside together. They had few responsibilities, but when Mom needed walnuts for baking, it was their job. They broke walnuts outside on the cement slab in front of the garage. Sometimes they carried water in from the pump, but I don't remember seeing them work in the house. Maybe it was easier and less stressful for Mom when Lorna helped her, and Jean, Irene, and I stayed outside.

One day, Irene stepped on a board with a nail sticking out of it, and the nail went through her foot. I was away from the house and missed seeing it. My mother drove her into town to the doctor's office.

I remember hearing the folks talk afterward—they were upset because they didn't have the money on hand to pay for the visit. I'm sure they figured out a way to come up with the two- or three-dollar fee. That's the only family injury I remember where the folks had to pay for a doctor.

During my high school years, football sent me to the doctor three times. Each time I went to the doctor's office on my own and paid for it with money I'd earned. The folks never had any insurance.

I once twisted my ankle severely while playing football. Dr. Scott taped it up and charged me about twenty-five dollars.

Another time, I cracked my ribs. I needed an x-ray, so it ended up costing more than my ankle injury. Doctor Scott wrapped tape around my midsection and told me to stay home for a few days. I stayed home and rested on the couch. When a friend came into the room once to visit, he made me laugh, and it almost killed me.

When I hurt my back, I tried the chiropractor. I knew it would be less expensive than the medical doctor. He heated my back, rubbed it down, and it felt pretty good. The office charged me ten or fifteen dollars. I'm thankful the doctors were able to help me out, but even more grateful that I stayed healthy overall except for those football injuries and contracting the measles.

Chapter 18

The Neighbors

Elwin and Ida Farmer

WHEN I WAS YOUNG AND we lived on the farm, my parents sometimes went dancing on Saturday nights with Elwin and Ida Farmer. The four of them often drove over to Soddy's in Lake Park. Soddy's was a restaurant, but on Saturday nights, the owners opened their dance floor of about twelve by twelve feet.

In his early performance years, Lawrence Welk frequently entertained at Soddy's. He played his accordion, accompanied by a small three- or four-member band. They played polkas and the schottische. Later, when my folks ran the Orleans Ballroom, Lawrence Welk performed there with a full orchestra.

I remember one Halloween when I went to the Farmers' house with the folks. It's the only time I ever went inside their home. They lived on the west side of Spirit Lake by the Rock

Island Depot. I really admired their heavy oak pocket doors between rooms. I also admired their sons, especially their youngest.

Kenny Farmer was their eldest son. His grandpa owned a farm and a gravel pit on the east side of Spirit Lake. During the war, Kenny drove a gravel truck. He stopped for his meals at Mom's café every day. Sometimes twice a day.

His brother Donny Farmer was a terrific basketball player. I enjoyed watching Don play. One afternoon, some servicemen came and pulled Don out of school. He got drafted right out of high school before he had the chance to graduate. Up until then, I hadn't realized that was a possibility. I heard Donny married after the war, but I never saw him afterward.

Ralph and Alice Brumm

Another couple, Ralph and Alice Brumm, lived down about a quarter of a mile from us and across the road. I went to their house with the folks once when I was about seven. They were sitting in the kitchen with their daughter Barbara. A small style of pot-bellied stove stood in the middle of the room. It was red hot and made of very thin metal.

Ralph Brumm sat in his kitchen with a dozen metal ice picks with wooden handles in a bucket by his feet. Everybody had them—they were used to chip ice off an ice block. Ralph, a big, tall, rugged-looking guy, sat there throwing ice picks at the back door, which was about fifteen feet from where he sat. One after another.

All night as they talked, Ralph threw ice picks at the door, retrieved them, then started again.

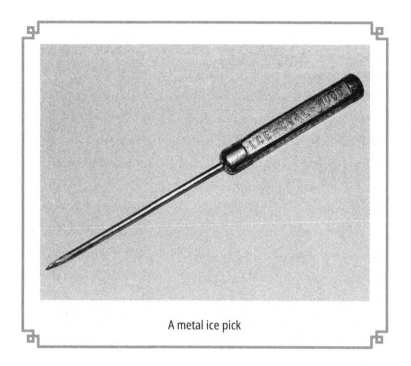

A metal ice pick

Their daughter Barbara was a little younger than me and a nice girl. We went into one of the bedrooms, and she opened the closet door. Ralph must have played the coronet because I saw one in the closet. I never did get the chance to play an instrument, but I sometimes thought about how great it would be to be able to play the coronet.

That's the only time I went inside the Brumms' house to visit. The folks went more, but I was stuck staying home with my sisters.

Dad and I rode to town with Ralph Brumm once. He enjoyed driving fast in his big car and slid all around those gravel roads. I didn't know if we were going to survive.

The Brumms had hosted dances in their empty barn haymow. I loved listening to the small bands, the fiddlers, and the man calling out the dances. Each time they hosted a gathering,

I got to have a bottle of orange pop. That was a huge deal for me. My sisters would dance, but I was too young. I'm not sure what kind of pop they got to drink. Maybe grape.

Ralph's dad owned the farm north of us. He bought another farm adjacent to his so Ralph could farm it. But Ralph preferred the fast life. It turned out that farming wasn't his thing. However, I can tell you that I sure would've loved it if my dad could have bought me a farm.

During the time the folks lived on the farm, they somehow got away once to take a trip with the Brumms. The four of them drove together to the Black Hills. The folks said Ralph and Alice loved it out there. I'm sure the four of them talked a lot about the farm and business on their vacation.

Since Ralph disliked farming, he persuaded my folks to leave our farm and partner together to run the Orleans Ballroom and Supper Club. But the Brumms liked the Black Hills so much that they left the partnership after a year. They moved to the Black Hills and started a business there. My folks seem to understand and parted from them on good terms. The Brumms returned to Spirit Lake several years later, and Alice ran a restaurant in downtown Spirit Lake.

Ralph liked to fly planes. During the Second World War, he joined the United States Air Force and became a flight instructor for new recruits. One day, he was in the air with a young guy. According to Ralph, the kid froze on the controls, and they crashed. Ralph survived, but he was badly injured. Besides broken bones, his face was all cut up and scarred for the rest of his life. Despite how wounded he was in the war, I found out recently that Ralph Brumm lived into his nineties, so I guess you never know.

Shimmy and Flo Damm

When we were on the farm, Shimmy and Flo Damm rented Shirks' farm across the road. When my folks first married, they had lived there. Before I was born, my sisters lived there too. Years later, my sister Jean told me it was a much nicer house, and she liked living there a lot more than on my grandpa's farm.

Shimmy and Flo claimed to be farming, but I never saw any evidence of it. My dad knew Shimmy wasn't interested in farming, so he rented a field from him. Dad raised alfalfa or timothy grass there. When the cows came in at the end of the day, he spread the hay in the manger in front of the stalls, and they would eat as Dad milked them. Otherwise, they just ate grass out in the pasture.

Shimmy was a bootlegger. That was common knowledge. Instead of spending his time farming, he spent it bootlegging. Dad told me that Shimmy drove to the dances on Saturdays and sold what he'd made. Some guys would bring a pint container hidden in the inner pocket of their jackets. Shimmy sold his wares out in the parking lot.

When Shimmy made enough money bootlegging, he opened up the Wonder Bar. That was around the time the laws changed and serving beer was allowed. When Shimmy opened the Wonder Bar for business, my folks went there once because they were neighbors.

Mom and Dad brought me along, and we sat at a booth. Shimmy brought the folks each a glass of beer. He gave me my own small glass of beer, about twice the size of a shot glass. That's the first beer I'd ever tasted. I was about five years old.

Shimmy was a friendly, outgoing guy. Because he'd gone around to all the dance halls selling booze, he knew the drinkers in the area. Everyone seemed to like Shimmy. No one ever re-ported him to the police for his bootlegging, as far as I know.

People didn't drink to excess. They didn't get so drunk that they couldn't drive. Most people just had a drink or two and drove carefully home. Spirit Lake was a small city, and car wrecks almost never happened. People didn't end up in the ditch because of getting drunk and driving. It didn't happen like it does now. Of course, we drove on country roads, not a four-lane highway. And people took their time going home.

Shimmy and Flo ran the Wonder Bar for several years. After a while, they sold it and built a nightclub at the end of the road, right by the pump house. It was a fancy two-story establishment about two blocks from where we lived. He hired a hostess—a woman from Spirit Lake in her thirties who knew everybody. The business did well for a year or two, but then it stopped being successful. And then the place burned down.

Shimmy was quite an operator. He had that nightclub going well. I don't know why his success didn't last. Maybe the location wasn't as good as it would have been down on West Okoboji. Businesses there have the advantage of attracting both locals and summer trade.

Shimmy really got around. He did all that bootlegging, plus he ran three different businesses. I was pretty young when the folks took me with them to the Twin Lakes, where Shimmy was building a new nightclub. When we approached, we saw that the lake was dry. The state had drained it to deal with the carp. The lake was a mudhole, and Shimmy's new place wasn't open yet. It had been a rare spur-of-the-moment trip for the folks to see Shimmy and Flo and the new place. It's too bad it didn't work out.

The Fricks

One time Dad went to bring our cows up, and he found our pasture full of bison. Well, they were bison, but we all called them buffaloes. Jake Frick was our neighbor on our side of the road on the east toward Spirit Lake. Buffaloes that Jake was paid to care for had wandered over from his land and knocked our fence down.

Dad drove over to talk to Jake. They made an agreement that Jake could keep them in our pasture until he found a permanent spot. Jake and Dad eventually got the animals where they belonged and repaired the fence.

Dad and I drove to their place once. Three of the boys were taking a shower outside but couldn't be seen from the road. They had fastened a metal washtub with plenty of holes in the bottom up high. One boy got under the shower, and the other two threw buckets of water into the tub. They took turns getting a shower that way.

The family didn't have a barn, just a house and a couple of small buildings. Emmet, the oldest boy, was out of school and had left the farm. He worked at the local hardware store. The second oldest boy was full of mischief and often caused trouble, according to Jean and Irene.

Jake eventually moved with his family to a very nice farm north of Estherville. When we were hunting in the area, Dad drove past it to show it to me.

Chapter 19

Selling Corn

ONE YEAR WHEN GRANDPA DAVE hauled a load of field corn to the Spirit Lake elevator with his Model T Ford truck, I rode along. The truck box wasn't large compared to later truck models. It was closer to the size of a pickup box.

At the elevator, workers weighed the truck carrying the load of corn. Once they unloaded the corn crop, the workers weighed the empty truck, subtracting the difference to get the corn weight. Before they paid Grandpa, they measured the moisture of the corn. The lower the moisture, the more money they paid per bushel.

After that day, Grandpa Dave and Dad decided to build a corn crib. Corn cribs were used to dry and store field corn on the ear. The field corn would later be used for animal feed.

Dad and Grandpa mixed their own cement and used it to make a concrete base for the building. They cut down several trees and trimmed them. Next, they set up and operated a big saw, running a belt from a pulley on the tractor.

Once they finished the corn crib, it held corn on each side—like a shed with thick walls—and offered a place to park farm equipment in the center of the building. The openings between the boards on each side of the crib allowed air to circulate through the corn to dry it. Now, by drying their corn crop properly before taking it to the elevator to sell, Dad and Grandpa could earn a higher price per load.

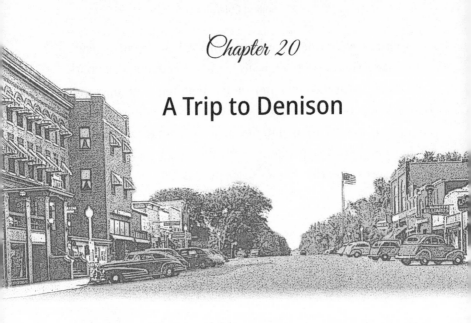

Chapter 20

A Trip to Denison

GRANDPA DAVE TOOK ME ALONG to keep him company when he drove to Denison, Iowa, to visit his daughter Fern and her husband, Bill Grosshans. Denison was known as the hometown of actress Donna Reed. The town is straight south of Lake Park, Iowa, halfway between Sioux City and Omaha, Nebraska, only east into Iowa.

When we arrived in Denison, it seemed like a busy town to me. We pulled up to a huge grocery store where Bill was the store manager, and Fern worked at the check-outs.

On our trip back, we stopped in a town and visited Mabel Higley in her home. She was a cousin and close friend of Grandma Maude. Mabel Higley owned a large parrot that she kept in a big cage. If the parrot said, "Polly want a cracker," then Mabel gave the bird a small cracker. It was the first parrot I'd ever seen, and it made a big impression.

I wasn't told why Grandpa made the trip, but a short time later, Bill and Fern came to Spirit Lake and moved in with my grandparents. I overheard that the store had been sold, and the new owner chose to run it himself. When Bill and Fern lived with Grandpa and Grandma, their Chow Chow dog stayed on Grandpa's back porch. That dog tried to attack me every time I entered the house.

Grandpa Dave and I had gone to Denison that day in his large car, a Willys-Knight. He ended up selling it in 1952 and purchasing a 1950 Pontiac.

When my cousin Maxine was learning to drive, she'd driven the Willys-Knight right through the front of the garage. When Grandpa repaired his garage, he added length to it. Later, he ended up needing the extra room for his Pontiac.

In 1953, on the day my wife and I left for our honeymoon, the door fell off my car, so Grandpa Dave loaned us his Pontiac for our honeymoon trip.

He drove that Pontiac until the time of his death in 1960.

When Bill and Fern moved to Spirit Lake from Denison, they started a boat livery business at Arnolds Park. Anyone crossing the bridge to the park that divided East and West Okoboji would have seen the livery located to the west, right on West Okoboji Lake.

Bill and Fern's boat livery business only lasted for one summer. After that, Bill worked at Grandpa Dave's livery.

One time, Bill decided to drive to Las Vegas and make his fortune. He loaded up his car with gambling equipment, including a roulette wheel. He wasn't gone much more than a week before he ran out of money and returned to Spirit Lake.

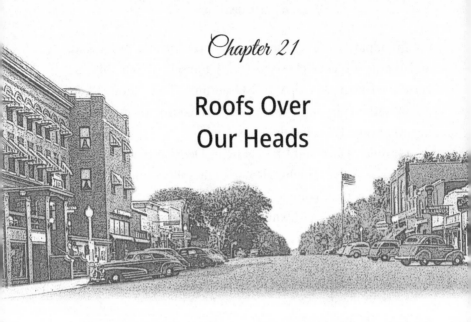

Chapter 21

Roofs Over
Our Heads

M Y OLDER COUSIN WAYNE FRONK and his sister Maxine lived with their mother in Woonsocket, South Dakota. Woonsocket is a small town north of Mitchell, halfway to Huron. Their mother, Margie, my dad's older sister, had married a Fronk from Orleans, Iowa. Then later, they divorced.

When I was seven years old, Grandpa Dave took me along when he drove to Woonsocket. It must have been after Margie's second husband, Alvin Jensen, was killed. I believe that was the reason for the trip. Alvin Jensen worked for the railroad company. He happened to be struck by a train while driving his car past a railroad crossing. Margie had just had a baby, so it must have been a terrible time for her. The baby, Tommy, must have been sleeping in a bedroom—I never saw him during our visit.

Margie, Wayne, Maxine, and the baby lived in town in a modest home that was not well-built. On windy days, sand found its way inside because of the cracks around the windows and the doors.

Woonsocket was a small town with a square. In the middle of the square was a swimming pool fed by an artesian well. It seemed as if every kid from miles around was at the pool. Wayne and I swam there together. By that time, I was a pretty good swimmer, having learned the year before. I enjoyed going off the diving board in Woonsocket, but I was afraid to try the thirty-foot platform.

On our trip back, Grandpa drove past the Sioux Falls prison so I could get a look at it. We also drove to the west end of Sioux Falls and walked through the zoo together. That was my first experience ever visiting a zoo.

When Wayne graduated from high school, there were no jobs available in Woonsocket, so he came to Spirit Lake and stayed with our grandparents. My aunt Fern and her husband already lived with them. And Wayne's sister Maxine had moved in earlier and occupied the other spare bedroom. No extra rooms were available at Grandpa Dave and Grandma Maude's house, so Wayne had to sleep in the most unusual place.

Grandpa hung a curtain partition between a small open space between the door and the bathtub in the only bathroom in the house. The stool and sink were set deepest in, along the back wall. My grandparents set up a cot in the entrance area of the bathroom, and Wayne slept there. At night, anyone entering or leaving the bathroom had to walk past Wayne, with only the curtain separating his cot from the toilet.

Later, Grandpa fixed up a room over the livery boat house for Wayne. The livery had no electricity or running water, and Wayne had to use the outdoor toilet. Soon after, the state built a nice outdoor his-and-hers bathroom facility adjacent to the boathouse and next to the spillway.

After leaving Woonsocket because her husband had died, Margie (Dad's sister) was at Grandma and Grandpa's house a lot. She shared a bed with her daughter, Maxine. From there, she moved near Jackson, Minnesota, where she rented a large two-story house. Older people who could no longer manage living on their own paid her monthly to rent a room. There weren't nursing homes or assisted living places such as there are now. Older people often moved in with one of their children. Margie provided a place for the older people to live who didn't have children to help them. Each person got their own room, and Margie provided the meals. On warm weather days, the lodgers could sit outside on the large front porch.

I visited her there once. Wayne and Maxine never lived with her there. Margie's son, Tommy Jensen—from her second husband—found a job in Spencer when he was older. He sometimes came to Spirit Lake to visit Grandpa Dave and Grandma Maude.

Maxine still lived with my grandparents for a while after Wayne moved to the boathouse. My dad's sister Fern and her husband, Bill Grosshans, were there too. But Bill died of a heart attack at the young age of thirty-six.

When my grandma Maude died in 1946, Fern remained in the house with Grandpa Dave. She never remarried. In the last years of Grandpa's life, Fern took care of him. After he passed away in 1960, Fern sold the house and rented an apartment in town.

Chapter 22

Seven Homes in Two Years

WHEN OUR FAMILY LEFT THE farm, we moved into two of the five empty rooms over Grandpa Dave's boat livery. We stayed there without electricity or a bathroom for a couple of weeks until my folks could find a place to rent. While we lived in the boathouse, we used the nearby outdoor state facility toilets. We ate our meals at the Sail Inn, the restaurant the folks ran below the Orleans Ballroom.

During the next two years, our family lived at seven different addresses. I always walked to school during the two years we lived in town.

After the rooms at the boat livery, we rented a house one block west of the electric generating plant of Spirit Lake. Jerry and Lorna moved from Milford and took half the house. The large diesel engines of the nearby plant generated electricity for the town. Whenever the generators started up, they shook the whole house.

The one-story home had an unusual number of windows. Whenever the dwelling shook, the windows rattled. None of us could sleep, so we left the place as soon as the folks could find another rental.

They soon found a two-story home on Hill Avenue about three blocks north of town on the east side of the street. We lived in the downstairs, and Lorna and Jerry took the upstairs. There was only one kitchen, but Mom was at the restaurant all day, so Lorna often had the kitchen to herself.

Lorna and Jerry moved out after a while. I think it was because the rent was more than they thought they could afford, but my folks never discussed the details with me.

Dad came back from town one day with a bike for me. The twenty-eight-inch bike had large, thin wheels. He had bought it for two dollars from a guy who needed money. Dad walked along, holding the bike while I peddled. I wasn't able to reach both peddles at once. I leaned to one side and then to the other. After a few tries, I could ride alone, see-sawing back and forth, but the bike was never a pleasure to ride.

Next, we moved to an apartment by the back door of the one-story Marion Hotel. When I was home alone, I spent time bouncing a basketball off one of the walls. A dog trainer who came to Mom's restaurant had given me the new ball. Neighbors complained to the folks, so I stopped. While we were there, our old dog Tricksy developed a large growth on one front leg. It got so bad that they took her to the vet, and he had to put her to sleep. Tricksy was older than Lorna, and Lorna was twenty years old at the time.

A larger apartment became available, so we moved to a different apartment at the Marion Hotel. I came down with measles while we lived there. I remember the day Grandpa

Dave came to visit me. I was secluded in a small bedroom with the shades pulled and no light. Mom said the measles could affect my eyesight, so it was important to shield my eyes from sunshine and light.

Around that time, my grandma (Minnie Baker) took a small two-bedroom apartment toward the front of the Marion Hotel. She told me she got tired of trying to do everything at the house by herself. I could enter through a side door of the hotel and be close to her door. Sometimes after school, I'd stop and play Chinese checkers and visit with her.

Grandma told me she read her Bible every day. Her favorite passage was: "In my Father's house are many mansions; if it were not so, I would have told you. I go to prepare a place for you. And if I go and prepare a place for you, I will come again, and receive you unto myself; that where I am, there ye may be also" (John 14:2–3 KJV). She quoted it often to me.

When it was her birthday or another special day, I would buy her a handkerchief. I found out after her death that she kept them but never used them. My grandma gave me several 1800 series coins, which I later passed down to my children.

After the hotel, the folks rented an apartment on the west side of the same street, one block east of Hill Avenue. The place was across from a business that raised and sold baby chickens. A couple of times while we were there, the hatchery business paid two men from Japan to separate the male chicks from the female chicks. No one in the area could do it.

The house was brick, and the landlady lived downstairs. She was divorced, and her former husband lived in a small cottage on the east side of Spirit Lake near Omar's Boat Livery. He worked as a mason.

At first, we didn't have an icebox, so we kept our milk cold in a windowsill. Later, when the folks bought an icebox, an iceman would deliver a cake of ice and place it in the top of the icebox. A tray underneath collected water as the ice melted.

Later, we took an apartment in the lower half of a house close to Highway 9, about three blocks east of the business district, on the northeast corner of that street.

After that, the folks rented a small house in Orleans, across the road from the lake. The population of Orleans at that time was about 200. Besides the school, the post office, and the grocery, there were cottages along the lake, plus the Orleans Ballroom and the well-known Orleans Hotel. The cottages and hotel drew summer tourists interested in swimming, fishing, and boating on the lakes.

Chapter 23

Mom's Restaurant

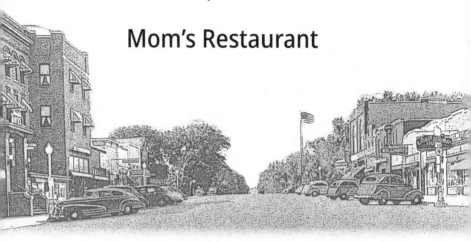

AFTER RALPH AND ALICE BRUMM moved to South Dakota, the folks were on their own managing the Orleans Ballroom and Supper Club. Business was going well. The Iowa Great Lakes region was a magnet for big bands—they all played there. The dances were big, and plenty of people ate at the supper club below.

The couple who owned the ballroom also owned the well-known Orleans Hotel and a number of cottages along the lake. When the man died, his widow continued as landlord. She could see the crowds the ballroom drew, so she kept raising the rent. She finally raised it so high that the folks couldn't make a living with it anymore and had to quit. I'm sure it was difficult for the folks to lose the ballroom and supper club after their struggles with the farm, but they never discussed financial matters in front of me. I didn't ask, and they never shared.

The landlord never did get anybody to run the ballroom who could make a success of it again. They pulled in a fairly good crowd on a few Saturday nights, but it was never again as successful as when the folks ran it.

Mom opened a restaurant by the shores of Big Spirit Lake in 1938. She called it Neil's Café. It stood on the south end of Big Spirit Lake in Orleans, Iowa, across the street from the Orleans Ballroom they had managed. When I wasn't in school, I spent my time at or near Mom's café so she could keep an eye on me. I ate my meals at the counter. If Mom wasn't busy, she would sit on a chair on the other side of the counter to keep me company. We didn't enjoy regular family meals around the table anymore as we had done on the farm. I missed that.

My folks purchased the restaurant with a rent-to-own type of arrangement. First, they bought the restaurant, and later we moved into the cottage. The cottage was right on the lakeshore, and the restaurant stood right behind it on the narrow piece of land between the lake and the road. The folks bought a CCC barracks in Milford that was no longer being used.

> The CCC (Civilian Conservation Corps) was a federal program during the Great Depression that offered work on environmental projects to millions of men.[2]

A trucking company moved the barracks to Spirit Lake and attached it to the back end of the restaurant, creating an L-shaped building. The part nearest our cottage was the old barracks. Mom placed a large freezer in there. This allowed her to buy meat in bulk ahead of time and remove it from the freezer as needed. The freezer was a game-changer for the restaurant.

---

2. "The Civilian Conservation Corps," National Park Service (website), retrieved May 30, 2023, https://www.nps.gov/articles/the-civilian-conservation-corps.htm.

The folks built a bathroom inside the restaurant too. Before that, there was an outside toilet behind the building.

Dad and I dug the septic system by hand and hooked it up to the restaurant and the house. That was a lot of work. Behind the restaurant where the outdoor toilet had been, we put in a huge cement pit. We dug a big drainage ditch going west, laid tiles down there, and laid roofing shingles over the cracks. We needed to dig across the small road between the cottage and the restaurant. Once we had dug down about four feet, we found mostly water because we were in between the two lakes: Big Spirit Lake and East Okoboji. Once the project was complete, we never had any trouble with drainage and never had to have it pumped out before the town came through and built sewers several years later. Of course, the DNR rules changed after we put in the system—they wouldn't allow anything similar near water nowadays.

Mom's restaurant had regulars who stopped in almost every day. A man who drove an ambulance from Des Moines used to come into the restaurant frequently. There must have been a lot of people going to Des Moines by ambulance because he drove back and forth all the time. His ambulance could hold just one person. It looked similar to a modern-day hearse—not like the big ambulance vehicles that are common now. I used to sit with him at the restaurant to hear about who he'd brought up to Spirit Lake or taken to Des Moines.

The ambulance driver always sat at the counter and ordered a hamburger steak. He used mustard instead of ketchup, and he ordered fried potatoes and a vegetable such as green beans or peas. A person could get a nice meal at the restaurant for cheap. I thought the hamburger steak was the best thing on the menu. Even now, my favorite meal is a well-done hamburger steak, potatoes, and peas or green beans—all served with a slice of bread.

Billy Moore was another regular. He came to this country from Germany and started a ranch out in Montana. He told us that after he built the ranch up, his wife got tired of him, and they divorced. She took the ranch, and he ended up in Milford, Iowa. He began to build and tend beehives around the countryside. His white beehive boxes could be seen all over. He owned his own truck, so whenever he collected enough honey, he drove to Sioux City and sold it.

Billy owned a nice boat and trailer. He and the man who owned the dry cleaners started fishing together. After fishing, the two of them would often stop at Mom's restaurant, and I'd hear about what they had caught that day.

Billy told me that when he lived in Germany, inflation was terrible. He had to carry a basketful of money uptown to buy a loaf of bread. His mom had given him a needle and some heavy thread. He bent the needle, put a red piece of cloth on it, and went down to the river to catch fish. That's how he began to fish—so he and his mother could eat. He said he loved fishing from then on.

Fishermen would often come to the restaurant for a meal. I'd hear them identified as rich tourists from Omaha or Des Moines or Chicago. But no one ever left a tip, no matter how rich they were. I don't think my mom or anyone working at the restaurant ever got a tip the entire time she owned the place.

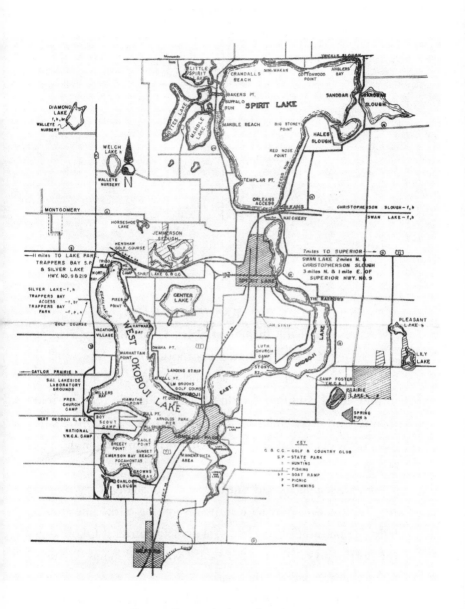

Iowa Great Lakes Region

Chapter 24

Frankenstein

I HEARD ABOUT THE MOVIE *FRANKENSTEIN* when it was showing at the theater in Spirit Lake, and I was eager to see it. I kept pestering my mother about how much I would love to watch the movie. One Saturday, she finally gave in and said I could go. I didn't have my bicycle yet, so I had to walk the three miles to town, then walk back to the café after the movie. The show started in the late afternoon or early evening.

Frankenstein turned out to be an unusually scary movie. By the time the show let out, it was getting dark. The streetlights helped until I reached Gilbert Park on East Okoboji at the north end of town. After that, I walked alone in darkness along the right side of the road.

As I passed the trees on the edge of Gilbert Park, I was convinced someone or something must be lurking behind each one of them. There was very little traffic, so car lights didn't offer much help.

When I was a young boy on the farm, my sisters had almost scared me to death when the folks were gone on Saturday nights. Those experiences, combined with the scary movie I'd just seen, conspired against me.

I tried to pick up my pace, but I was too frightened to get up much speed. Once darkness fell, everything seemed fearsome. And nothing changed the entire hike home.

My walk back to the restaurant after the movie that night frightened me so much that it made a big impression on me. I've never forgotten *Frankenstein* or that long walk in the dark. And I was never so glad to be back at the café in my life. That was the end of my movie days for a long time.

....

SPIRIT LAKE'S GILBERT PARK ON Hill Avenue, previously called Chautauqua Park, was renamed in 1926 in honor of Fred "Dood" Gilbert. Gilbert was raised on a farm near Spirit Lake.

He became one of Spirit Lake's most famous residents by winning shooting contests. Gilbert, also known as "The Wizard of Spirit Lake," was a master of the shotgun—a talented trap shooter and a pretty big deal around the lakes area when I was young. Shooting contests were common. In addition to local contests, he won contests around the country and internationally too.

In 1902, he made a run of 200 straight targets without a miss. Three years later, he broke his own record by scoring 402 targets. In 1919, still undefeated, he broke his own record again by shooting 591 in a row. Shotguns used to have a big kickback, so he must have been awfully black and blue.

Composer John Philip Sousa, well-known for his marching band music, was friends with "Dood" Gilbert. Sousa began trap shooting in the early 1900s and received instruction from Gilbert. My dad found out that in exchange, Sousa gave Gilbert bass drum lessons. Gilbert struggled to play well, so Sousa suggested some tricks, including spitting in order to time a pause, to help Gilbert play the drum well enough to participate in the town's marching band.

Chapter 25

JayDee Ferguson

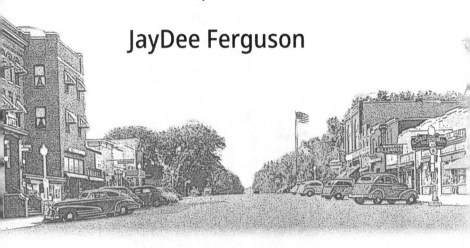

WHEN MOM AND DAD AND the Brumms ran the Orleans Ballroom and Lawrence Welk played there on Saturday nights, the folks must have had a contract with him. He played other places, but they had him tied up on Saturday nights. Cars filled the gravel parking lot during the era when he had a full-sized orchestra performing with him, not just a polka band. Other bands played there on Wednesdays, but Lawrence Welk drew a good crowd every Saturday.

The folks must have sold a lot of suppers downstairs at the Sail Inn before the Saturday dances. It was always busy. Before they opened, Mom would make our dinner and we sat together to eat. I would eat my early supper there and then head outside. Those were exciting times.

Lawrence Welk, 1940s

On Saturday nights, JayDee Ferguson and I climbed a big tree by the northeast corner of the upstairs dance hall. That's where the bands played, close to the lakeshore. Only adults were allowed upstairs in the ballroom, but we could see the musicians and hear the music well from our spot in the tree. We spent a lot of time there.

My favorite song was "Josephine." I loved when they played it. I heard Lawrence Welk's orchestra perform the song many years later on television, and it sounded just the same to me.

JayDee Ferguson was a neighborhood boy four years older than me. During the summer months, he and his mom stayed in a cottage on the lake in Orleans, not far from the ballroom. His father owned a three-chair barbershop in Spencer and would join the family on weekends. Many vacationers did that sort of thing. During the summers when I was nine and ten years old, JayDee and I spent a lot of time together swimming, fishing, and having adventures.

When it was mealtime, his mom would step outside and yell JayDee's name. Even if we were about a block away over at the livery boathouse, we could hear her plain as day. She called, and JayDee went running. I never saw the inside of his home, and he never saw mine. But between meals, we spent our days together out of doors.

Tommy Moen, a biologist for the State of Iowa, spent time with the two of us one day. He taught us that we could swim much faster when we were underwater—about twice as fast—if we swam on our sides with the arm stroke and kick he taught us.

Every summer, a woman who had been a champion in the Olympic Games came to the area and swam across the lake. The swim from starting point to finish was a distance of five miles. JayDee Ferguson and I decided we'd swim across, but we didn't tell anyone our plan. When we were more than half-way across, someone told my dad we were swimming in the middle of Spirit Lake. Dad ran and grabbed one of Grandpa's livery boats and rowed out to where we were. He told us to get in the boat. That was a huge disappointment. We were doing fine and were confident we could have made it to the other side. We never tried it again.

I was eleven when my parents sent me away for the summer to help Jerry and my sister Lorna on their farm. I wasn't home that entire summer, and JayDee and I lost track of each other after that.

....

YEARS LATER WHEN I WAS a freshman at the university, our team traveled to a track meet in Nebraska. We arrived at the meet, and I noticed JayDee Ferguson's name on the roster. He was easy to recognize. We talked, and he said he was going to run the high hurdles. I told him I'd be pole vaulting. He had been in the Army and was going to college on the G.I. Bill. It was exciting to see JayDee again.

Chapter 26

Selling Night Crawlers

MOM'S RESTAURANT, GRANDPA DAVE'S BOAT livery, the Orleans Ballroom, and our cottage on the lake were all situated near each other, near the present site of the spillway between Big Spirit Lake and East Okoboji. The ballroom stood right across the road from the lake and the other three buildings, not far from the Spirit Lake Fish Hatchery building. The rest were on the lake side of the road.

A nice-looking dog trainer in his thirties often stopped at Mom's café. He trained black Labrador retrievers for hunting. Several times, he brought a certain female retriever with him to the restaurant. She was the best-behaved and most well-trained dog I've ever been around. If he told the dog to lie down, she stayed put until given the order to move. On command, the dog crouched and crawled wherever the trainer told her to go. She rolled over across the room until told to stop.

One time, the man threw a piece of hamburger to the dog and said, "Hold." About ten minutes later, after some conversation, he said, "Okay, you can eat it."

I think the trainer liked me because he and his wife didn't have their own kids. One time he bought me a new basketball. It was leather with leather strings on one side and seemed to be a top-notch ball.

That's the ball I bounced off the wall in the small apartment at the back of the Marion Hotel and got the angry complaint from a next-door neighbor.

Later, the trainer bought me two pairs of leather boxing gloves. I got enthused about boxing but had a hard time finding anyone willing to box with me. The next year, I was able to make good use of them though. I'll save that story for a later chapter.

Another salesman who came to the restaurant once gave me a bat and ball, so I did pretty well with equipment.

That year, I began going out at night to pick up night crawlers as a way to earn my own money. There were plenty of fishermen in the area willing to pay for bait. I often went out searching, especially after a rain. A couple of times when I first started out, my folks helped me when we returned to Spirit Lake after they closed the restaurant for the night.

During the summer, I posted a sign at the rear of the restaurant:

NIGHT CRAWLERS FOR SALE
25 CENTS PER DOZEN

Later, my price went up to fifty cents per dozen.

Dad gave me two large wooden fish boxes. I filled them with dirt and placed night crawlers in them. I fed them used coffee grounds from the restaurant and dandelion leaves. I began to manufacture almost all my worms in the two boxes.

Things went so well that I started to sell my worms to boat liveries. There were a number of boat liveries in the area. Two were nearby, on the same street as the restaurant.

I earned five dollars per gallon of worms. Later, I was able to raise the price to six dollars per gallon. When I was eleven years old and gone from home for the entire summer, the folks continued to sell the worms for me and let me keep the profits.

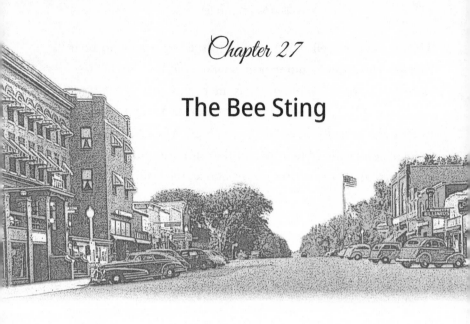

Chapter 27

The Bee Sting

I STOOD ON THE LAKESHORE ABOUT fifty yards east of our white cottage on Big Spirit Lake. As I threw flat stones across the water, I counted how many times I could get them to skip across the surface before they sank.

Without warning, I felt a bee sting me on the head. At the same time, I heard a zip and saw a splash out in the lake. My mind didn't connect the zip with the splash. Fish often splashed in the lake, so it didn't seem unusual.

Smarting from the sting, I went and found my dad and told him what had happened. Later that day, Dad walked over and had a talk with our nearest neighbor, Frank Marnett.

Frank was a well-known fisherman and pretty famous in the area. The *Spirit Lake Beacon*, the local newspaper, dubbed him the "dean of Spirit Lake fishing." Frank Marnett's place was located near the highway on the strip of land between the road and the lakeshore. He owned a little shop downstairs in the front of the building, and he lived above it. He sold fishing tackle, hooks, and line. He also made bamboo fishing poles and terrific plugs from balsam wood that wouldn't sink.

Locals and vacationers often stopped in at his shop for advice about where to fish. On one occasion, I went upstairs and got a look at his living quarters. The entire front area held stacks and stacks of magazines and newspapers. He spent a lot of time reading about fishing and that sort of thing.

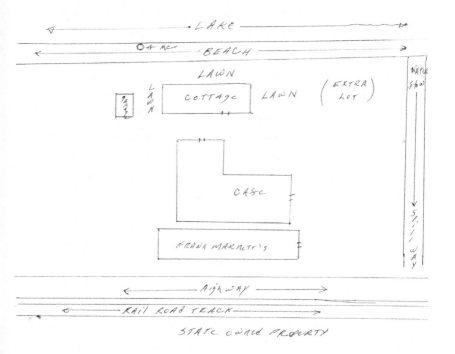

Mom's café was close by, also between the road and the lake. Our cottage was on the lake—behind Frank's place but several feet lower in elevation. It turned out that as I stood on the lakeshore skipping stones that day, Frank was behind his cottage with his .22 long rifle, shooting at rats. He had a problem with rats under his house because his place wasn't built on a cement slab. My dad figured out that one of the bullets must have grazed my head.

Another inch, and I wouldn't have survived.

....

FRANK MARNETT MADE FLY LURES that had a red head and a white body. Fish went crazy over them. It was the only thing I ever used.

One time, a bunch of older businessmen from Spirit Lake were out on the lake fishing. I stood out near them on a sandbar with my fly rod. I caught twenty-six silver bass in a row. It was too many to keep, and I felt pretty proud of myself. The older men caught a few, but nothing like I was catching.

Frank was smart when it came to fish. He made my bamboo pole. I've still got it. It's a six-foot pole that slides together. He taught me how to use the kind of reel that didn't have a level wind (which wraps the line evenly on a spool). For reeling the line in, Frank taught me to guide it back and forth, allowing me to cast a lot farther.

Today they sell these things where the line just falls off effortlessly. Frank Marnett had one in the forties. He had three of us guys trying it out. It was made in England. I don't know where he bought it, but if you go into any hardware store, that's what they sell now. The fisherman holds on to the line, and when he lets go, the line just falls off rather than the reel going around. If I'd had any business brains back then, I could have made a fortune because nobody in the area had them back then.

A local guy named Berkley Bedell had plenty of business brains. He said he learned how to tie a fly out at Frank Marnett's, and look what happened with him. He used that knowledge to build a fine, successful business. As a kid, he started paying local housewives to tie flies in their homes, and he sold them to tackle shops. His fishing tackle business did so well that he bought an old house first, and then he built a two-story factory in town. Later he built a big factory on the other side of the cemetery. Eventually, he had multiple factories going.[3]

---

3. Larry Ramey and Daniel Haley, *Tackling Giants: The Life Story of Berkley Bedell* 3rd edition (Winfield, KS: National Foundation for Alternative Medicine, 2005).

(left) Frank Marnett's home and tackle shop;
(right) Lorna's sons Bob and Dick in front of Mom's Café

Chapter 28

Dad's New Job

THE IOWA CONSERVATION COMMISSION HIRED my dad to seine carp from area lakes. Test seining had revealed a huge population of rough fish and relatively few game fish in comparison. Rough fish such as carp, buffalo, sheepshead suckers, and bullheads are not considered game fish.

Carp were introduced with good intentions in the late 1800s, but carp multiplied rapidly, threatened water quality, and destroyed game fish. They also wiped out forage fish, which affected local game bird populations. Carp can increase phosphorous levels, destroy plant communities, reduce water clarity, and basically wreak havoc.

The Iowa Conservation Commission declared war on carp. They concentrated efforts to eliminate carp through seining. Jobs were still tough to find, but I think I know how my dad got his foot in the door.

Seining is a type of fishing that uses nets. A seine is a fishing net with weighted sinkers on the bottom and cork floats along the top. Used by fishing crews from the shore or from a boat, the nets can be used to collect carp and other rough fish.

Back when Dad was still farming, the state had decided to create three or four large ponds on state property across the railroad tracks from Big Spirit Lake, close to East Okoboji. The state hatched walleyes at the fish hatchery every year and turned fingerlings loose into the lakes. Large fish were eating many of the newly hatched walleye.

The Commission decided to create ponds to give walleye fingerlings an opportunity to grow. They planned to seine them out once they grew and place them in the lakes so they might have a better chance to survive.

The state hired Dad and several other farmers to dig holes for the ponds. Dad owned a large scoop with wooden handles at each side. The front of the scoop had chains that allowed him to hitch it to his two horses. As the horses pulled forward, Dad held the handles up so the front of the scoop cut into the soil. When the scoop was full, the horses pulled it to the site, where Dad lifted the handles and dumped the soil out. The scoop was called a Fresno.

The conservation people found out he was a hard worker back in his farming days, and they must have remembered his work. I'm sure that's why they hired him. Dad was soon promoted to foreman. He worked as foreman of a seining crew for quite a few years.

The ponds the state built to help walleye fingerlings were a little bit of heaven for frogs, which always invaded the ponds.

There'd be little black tadpoles swimming around. Soon the three or four ponds were full of frogs. They probably preferred the small ponds rather than being out in the big lake.

Frogs are rare now, but there were all sorts of them around the lake when I was a kid, and they were easy to catch. I enjoyed eating frog legs. I used a paddle I'd made to knock them out. Then I carried the frogs to the restaurant in a burlap bag. After I cleaned them, mom cooked the legs for our family for supper. She'd cut a slit in one leg and stick a second leg through the slit so they wouldn't jump from the pan as she cooked them. Mom and Dad would eat a few, but I ate the majority, and they were delicious.

Chapter 29

School of Responsibility

WHEN MY FAMILY MOVED FROM Spirit Lake to Orleans, it meant we now lived in the Orleans school district. Orleans had their own small school that went up through the eighth grade, but I'd always attended school in Spirit Lake.

I told my parents I was not going to go to the Orleans school. Spirit Lake offered football, basketball, and track. The small Orleans school had no sports at all, and the kids I knew from Orleans swore a lot. I wasn't interested.

My folks drove to town and spoke with the school superintendent.

Mr. Ilsley said, "Neil can attend school here, but he can't ride the school bus since he lives outside the Spirit Lake school district."

My folks weren't available, so I needed to figure out my own transportation to school. My dad left early each morning to work for the Iowa Conservation Commission and my mother ran her restaurant. For Christmas, the folks and my grandpa had gone together and bought me a 24-inch bicycle. They each paid half. Until I turned sixteen years old, I rode my bicycle to school every day.

After my sixteenth birthday, I bought an old 1930 Model A Coupe. I paid for a driver's license, purchased insurance, and drove the car until it wasn't fixable. Then I sold it to the junkyard for twenty-five dollars.

Once in a while, I couldn't get to Spirit Lake for school because of the weather.

One time we had a huge storm. The lake we lived on was about five miles across.

The snow blew in across the lake so high that the snow-plow couldn't do anything. Orleans had to send for help to Des Moines. They brought up a special piece of equipment. There were huge buckets on the back of it that circled around. I think the machine threw the snow back into the buckets. Then workers hauled the snow away with trucks. I never saw the machine, but it must have been enormous. On the whole road in front of where we lived, the snow was as high as our house. There was no way anyone could get out.

I don't remember ever getting a ride, or walking, or missing school other than that big storm. Maybe I was sick once or twice, or maybe there was another snowstorm that kept me home. But not that I remember. I always rode my bike for the six-mile round trip.

. . . .

IN THOSE DAYS, THE SCHOOL provided free milk. All students would walk down to the cafeteria for a bottle of milk. Students could drink white milk, or they were given the option to add chocolate if they preferred chocolate milk.

The milkman delivered the standing order to the school building each morning. The milk bottles arrived in cases. Superintendent Ilsley assigned me to carry all the milk for the students into the cafeteria each day. I considered it an honor to be asked. I guessed that Mr. Ilsley was pleased I wanted to come to Spirit Lake for school, but I never really knew why he asked me.

The daughter of the man who ran the dry cleaners in town had a heart ailment. Because of her heart issues, she wasn't allowed to take the stairs. The school didn't have an elevator, so the young girl needed someone to carry her up and down the stairs. Mr. Ilsley assigned me the job.

A few years later, when they initiated a crossing guard program in front of the school, Mr. Ilsley appointed me in charge of the student crossing guards. I was responsible for deciding which students served on which days, when they would be relieved, and all other specifics of the crossing guard schedule.

I never knew for sure, but I assumed either Mr. Ilsley was pleased with my work, or he felt he could trust me. Maybe he felt I could use a boost of confidence.

In my senior year, I helped write the school yearbook. I suggested to our editorial team that we dedicate the yearbook to our school superintendent. I believed Mr. Ilsley was a great man and would be our best choice. Students at the meeting made a few other casual suggestions, but I insisted. The Spirit Lake High School Class of 1948 dedicated our yearbook to our school superintendent, Mr. Harry E. Ilsley.

Chapter 30

Men Without a Regular Trade

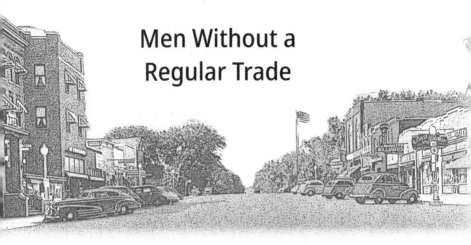

WHEN I WAS A KID, there were good, decent men in the area with families to support who didn't have a trade. Those men took whatever job they could find. Some relied heavily on hunting to feed their families. They shot rabbits, pheasants, and ducks. In deer season, they'd do their best to shoot a deer. Men without a trade who lived in the country had more opportunities to put food on the table for their families. If their land included a grove of trees, they were even more fortunate. They'd be more likely to find a deer that way. Deer were plentiful— they'd likely shoot one and butcher it whether it was in season or not.

Farmers had the benefit of land with which to garden. After we moved to the cottage, my dad made use of land across the street from the restaurant. I'm not sure if the State Conservation Commission owned it or the railroad—the railroad owned land on either side of the tracks. Either way, no one seemed to mind that my dad used the land to grow food.

97

Our neighbor, Frank Marnett, lived closer to the road. He grew tomatoes along the ditch near his cottage. The soil in the ditch was sandy, and his tomato plants did well.

Leo Kinniston lived in Spirit Lake in a small white house with his wife, Leona. Later on, the couple had children. Leo's house was sandwiched between the road and the railroad tracks. He hardly owned any land. He did plenty of hunting and fishing for food, but his lack of land presented challenges. Because of this, he needed to look for work wherever he could find it. Leo was a willing worker—he would do any odd job he could get. He's the one who came to the farm when the folks needed someone to make a horsehide blanket when Pony died.

Leo once told my dad that he'd tried to eat almost every animal a person could think of. He said he even tried fried skunk, but it had tasted so terrible he couldn't eat it.

Leo eventually found regular work with the State Conservation Commission. On the side, he drove a truck for a fish company to Big Stone Lake. One day, he picked up a load of carp to bring back that'd been seined through the ice.

A fierce snowstorm hit the area that day. Leo's truck fell through the ice and went down about twelve feet. He escaped from the cab, but he drowned. Apparently, he was unable to find the hole in the ice through which the truck plunged.

I've always felt terrible about that. Leo did everything he could while he was alive to take care of his family, and he never shirked any job.

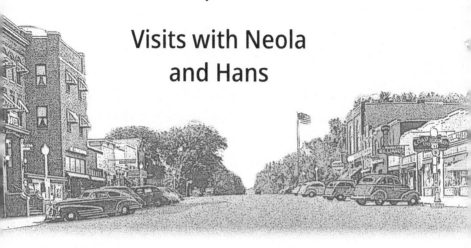

Chapter 31

Visits with Neola
and Hans

MY OLDER COUSIN NEOLA FROENDT asked my mother if I could visit for several days. My mom let me go with her. Neola loved children, and she and her husband, Hans, didn't have any. The two lived on a farm about four miles northwest of the town of Spirit Lake, a couple of miles west of Big Spirit Lake. Their farm was close to the farm where my grandmother Maude Swailes was raised before she married at the age of eighteen.

Neola was Aunt Kate's daughter, but she was close in age to my mother. Neola's mother, Kate, had died at the age of fifty-one due to an obstructed bowel. The doctors didn't diagnose the problem until it was too late to save her. Neola never fully recovered from her mother's death. She cried at the mention of her name for many years afterward.

Neola and Hans owned a player piano. I'd never seen one before. Neola inserted a roll. I was captivated as I watched the roll circle round. Protruding spikes hit something to cause piano keys to go down, resulting in the piano playing the intended song.

My first chore in the morning was to feed the chickens. I collected a basketful of ear corn and carried it to the hand sheller. I inserted an ear of corn, turned a long handle, and the inside parts rubbed the corn off the cob. I caught the kernels in a bucket and fed the shelled corn to the chickens. I don't remember what I was told to do with the cobs. I've heard that people used cobs for toilet paper, but I never knew of anyone who did.

After feeding the chickens, I watched Hans move hay, which he intended to use to feed the animals. I watered the chickens and went from one farm job to another. Neola was nice to me, but whenever I went into the house without Hans, she talked to me about her mother and cried. I wasn't sure what to say or how to respond.

On Saturdays back home, our folks always took us to Spirit Lake to shop. Neola and Hans went to Montgomery instead. It was my first time in Montgomery, and I enjoyed the adventure.

The big general store displayed a large Yager's sign out front. Yager's sold groceries, clothing, boots, and almost every item a farm family might need. Montgomery also had a schoolhouse, a grain elevator, a bank, a tavern, an ice cream shop, and a Case farm store. The size of Montgomery at that time was about as big as the town ever got. I don't think the population has grown to this date.

Montgomery, Iowa, showed movies outdoors on the side of the ice cream shop. People could sit on benches or inside their cars. I had a nickel or a dime that my mother had given me when I left home. At one point, I went into the ice cream store and ordered a vanilla cone. I took one bite from the top, and a big brown cockroach ran out. I went outside and threw the cone down. That was one of the greatest disappointments of my life. I'd spent all my money for ice cream and got nothing for it. I had never seen a cockroach, but I'd heard people talk about them, and somehow, I knew what it was. In spite of losing my cone, the trip to Montgomery was the highlight of my visit with Neola and Hans.

After the Wall Street Crash of 1929, small-town banks across the country were in trouble. My folks told me later that the banker in the little town of Montgomery took all the money from the bank one night, fled to Oklahoma by car, and never returned. I don't think Iowa had extradition from Oklahoma at the time.

My parents told me that after that happened, the farmers didn't trust the banks. They put their money in jars and hid them. The rock piles along the road weren't the only hiding places for jars. Sometimes, they'd bury jars by a tree. Bootleggers such as Shimmy Damm probably had liquor stashed in rock piles near the road too.

....

MY SECOND VISIT TO NEOLA and Hans resulted in a trip to Hutchinson, Minnesota. We visited Neola's brother Robert and his wife. Robert farmed just outside of Hutchinson, raising and selling beef cattle.

When we arrived, they were filling a silo with feed for their cattle. Robert's wife was dressed just as he was, wearing blue overalls and a blue overall jacket. She preferred working with him outside over cooking and housework. I had never seen that before. My parents had a more traditional division of labor. Dad did the outside work, and Mom took care of the inside work.

Robert and Tilly Browning had four children: Ruby, Leonard, Robert, and Betty. Leonard was the oldest boy, just younger than me. Betty was the baby in the wooden box in the middle of the room. Similar to the plain box for the baby, the rest of the furnishings weren't much to speak of. The meals were basic with nothing fancy, and we never had dessert.

The farm was good sized, with plenty that needed to be done. The three kids each had chores they were responsible for every day. I noticed that cleaning the house was low on the priority list.

For a treat, Neola took the four of us kids to a movie in Hutchinson. The theater was exceptionally nice compared to what I was used to. I had to go to the bathroom when we arrived, so I searched for a men's room sign but could only see signs for restrooms. I asked the other kids what a restroom was, and they said, "Don't you know a restroom is a toilet?" In my school, it was called a boys' room or a girls' room.

Robert told us at length about an agreement he had with a local banker who had loaned him money to purchase cattle. The banker was well-informed about cattle and advised Robert when to buy, when to complete the finishing (final feeding of the cattle), and when to sell. The banker read newspapers, magazines, listened to the radio, and talked with men in the cattle business. Robert was convinced he received excellent advice from him.

....

WHEN NEOLA AND HANS LIVED on the farm west of Big Spirit Lake, they bought a brand new two-toned 1936 coupe. They kept the car always looking as if it just came out of the showroom. Later on when they moved to town, they hardly ever drove it. They just kept the car in the garage. Hans died first, and Neola went into a nursing home.

A couple of times while I was visiting her, her nephew Leonard, Robert's son, was there with her. Neola left the car to him. Leonard became quite a mechanic. He later owned a business in Spirit Lake, where he repaired truck engines.

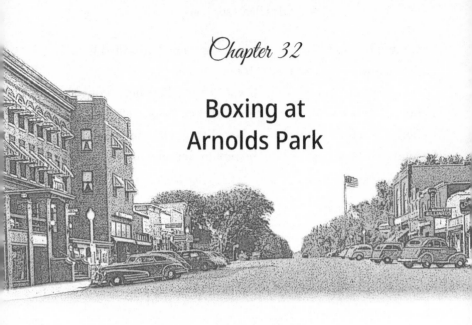

Chapter 32

Boxing at
Arnolds Park

I
N THE SUMMER OF 1939, my older cousin Wayne Fronk
started a softball team with other young men. They
played at the park in Spirit Lake—the one near East
Okoboji that used to have the big toboggan run. It's called
Memorial Park now.

I was thirteen years younger than Wayne and his friends. I
served as a bat boy, and I picked everything up for them. A lot
of older guys wouldn't have put up with having a younger kid
tagging along, but for some reason, Wayne and his friends did.
Wayne was good to me.

One Friday night, my cousin Wayne and a couple of his
softball friends took me to Arnolds Park, the local amusement
park. I thought it was pretty great that they let me tag along.
The Arnolds Park boxing ring was past the merry-go-round,
near the spot where you could earn an extra ride by pulling the
ring out of the lion while he was roaring.

Without discussing it and without asking me, Wayne signed
me up for the boxing preliminaries. The preliminaries were

three-round fights. I was only nine that year, but he marked me down as a twelve-year-old since entrants needed to be at least twelve to participate. I was excited about it.

I would have been scared to death to fight anybody, except that one year earlier, the dog trainer who always came to Mom's restaurant had given me those two sets of boxing gloves.

Good fighters traveled to Arnolds Park for the main bouts. Guys drove up from Sioux City and Chicago boxing clubs. Turp Boehm was local Spirit Lake talent. His reflexes were amazing—the quickest reflexes of anyone I ever saw. He made it to the final match of the Golden Gloves in Chicago, which was a big deal.

Once Wayne signed me up, I boxed all that summer at Arnolds Park against twelve- and thirteen-year-old boys. Two of my matches were draws, but the rest I won as technical knockouts (TKOs), which meant they stopped the matches before three rounds were over.

I remember fighting a kid from Chicago. He was left-handed, and I wasn't used to that. He beat me up for two full rounds before I figured out what to do. In boxing, you've got to figure out what the other guy is doing and then beat him at it. I faked with my left and hit quickly with my right. Wayne said he counted, and I hit the Chicago kid eighteen times with my right hand before they stopped the fight.

None of my school friends knew I boxed during the summers. I never told anybody. I don't think people from Spirit Lake attended the Arnolds Park matches—I never recognized anyone in the audience. I'm not sure if my folks ever knew I boxed. We never talked about it. Wayne may have eventually told them. I don't know. They were busy all the time with the restaurant, but they must have seen me across the road, training with the older guys.

The Lenox boys from Spirit Lake were super athletes. The two oldest Lenox boys were on the 1942 basketball team when Spirit Lake went to state. Bob played forward and was the team's high scorer. Ray played point guard, but right before the state games, Ray turned twenty and became ineligible to play. He must have been held back once due to illness or grades. He probably wasn't aware of the age-limit rule ahead of time. The coach was so upset when he found out Ray couldn't play at state that he wouldn't allow him in the team picture.

I trained with Ellis, the third oldest Lenox boy. He wasn't a great basketball player, but he was the heavyweight champion at Arnolds Park. When he wasn't boxing, he worked as a bouncer at Arnolds Park's biggest nightclub.

He and a couple of other guys trained over in front of the dance hall, across the way from Mom's restaurant. I just horned in and did what Ellis and the other guys did. We rolled on barrels to toughen our stomachs. We ran two miles out to the Orleans dump, running backward all the way to get our legs in shape for back-pedaling. We ran forward on the return. The older guys probably thought it was funny to see a little kid copying everything they did as they trained.

My reflexes were unusually quick, which helped later in basketball and football. Reach is important in boxing. Since I was younger and smaller, I needed to move quickly to get inside and hit. All that running to the dump came in handy. A boxer has to be able to move. Despite being quick on my feet, I was hit in the eyes and saw stars too many times to count.

Some of the farmers and other men who watched my matches said they liked the way I fought. They probably enjoyed seeing the smaller guy win. Some came up to me after I won, congratulated me, and handed me a fifty-cent piece or a silver dollar. Since the preliminaries were amateur fights, I shouldn't have accepted the coins, but I didn't know the rules at the time. And I liked earning the money.

One of Wayne's friends owned a four-door Model A. Whenever I won, the guys would put me up on the hood and drive through Arnolds Park, honking the horn the entire way. It was a great feeling.

Except for the summer when I was eleven, I boxed each summer until my sophomore year in high school. I have a hunch that Wayne signing me up for boxing was one of the best things that ever happened to me. It helped pull me out of my shell. Before I started the sport, I was quiet and kept most things to myself. I lacked the nerve to say much to anyone. Boxing helped me gain confidence.

Chapter 33

Paper Routes and Pin Setting

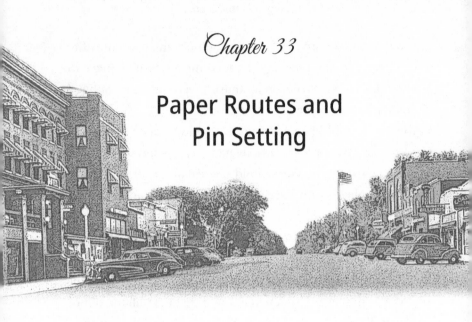

W HEN I WAS NINE, I started working two paper routes. I delivered *The Des Moines Register* Monday through Friday. On Saturday, I delivered *The Grit*, a national newspaper that came out only once a week. I earned five cents for each *Grit* paper that I sold, so it was a good money maker for me.

The *Des Moines Register* had to be delivered early in the morning before school. It was dark when I went out, and it was scary down by the railroad tracks. Men from out of town hopped on and off the train, so I never knew who was in town or whether it was safe or not. I could always see the hobos gathered around a barrel with a big fire in it.

Every week, I had trouble collecting money for the papers. Many of the women never had any money, so I'd have to bike uptown, find their husbands at their workplaces, and try to collect from them.

The bowling alley was located between town and the school. One day, I stopped and asked if they needed another pin setter. They hired me. I began to set pins for two alleys whenever the men's teams bowled. They paid me per lane. I kept both jobs until we moved to Orleans.

....

MY MOTHER BOUGHT ME THE sweater I wore when I graduated from junior high school. She also bought a heavy car coat for me when I turned sixteen. I still have that coat in my basement. Other than those two items, once I turned twelve years old, I needed to buy my own clothes, socks, underwear, and shoes. That year, I worked all summer on a seining crew for the State Conservation Commission. My dad helped me get that job.

Some kids I knew had to work to help their families put food on the table. Whatever money I earned that I didn't need for clothes, my parents allowed me to save. I'm not sure what inspired it, but I had a strong desire to save for college. My sister Jean went to beauty school, but no one in my family had ever graduated from college. I can't remember where the idea came from or why the plan took root.

From the time I started earning money, I was tight-fisted with it and did my best to save the majority of whatever I earned toward the goal of going to college after graduation.

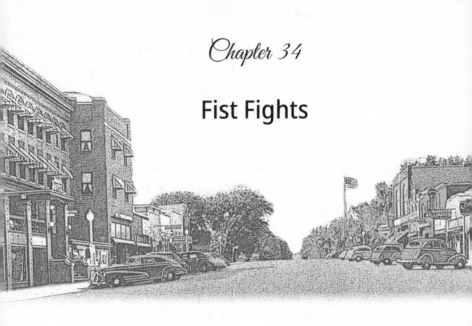

Chapter 34

Fist Fights

I NEVER WANTED TO GET INTO fights with other kids. I went out of my way to avoid conflict and arguments. But bullies can be hard to dodge. I was involved in two fist fights in my life, though I never wanted to have even one.

When I was eight years old, I walked past Harry Smith's house whenever going to and from school. We lived on Hill Avenue then, and my friend Harry lived with his family one block over. Harry's house was across the street from another boy in our class. Darrell was an only child of older parents and very mean. He was the type of boy who would pick up a rock and throw it at you when he was angry.

One day, an older boy who had just moved to town was with Harry and Darrell. I found out later that he was three grades ahead of us. Every time we spent time together, he told us stories about how he had been in fighting matches. He seemed to be fixated on the subject. He started saying he wanted to fight with me.

110

Harry had told him about the boxing gloves the dog train-er gave me. He'd given me two sets, but at that time, I hadn't even tried them on yet. Tired of hearing him say what a great fighter he was, I finally gave in.

"Okay, let's fight right now," I said.

He started hitting me, and I hit him back each time. After what seemed like a long time, we both got tired, and he stopped fighting. He never mentioned fighting to me again. Maybe we both learned a lesson.

....

YEARS LATER, JIM NORMAN, HARRY Smith, Dave Dean, and I decided to drive to the skating rink at Arnolds Park. It was November of our senior year in high school. We were to have our first basketball game the following week.

We thought we'd listen to the organ music from the side-walk outside of the rink and maybe go inside and watch people skate. Parking was right in front of the building by the sidewalk. We stood outside for a long time and then decided to go in.

Three of us were already inside, and when Jim Norman tried to come in the door behind us, a well-known bully from Arnolds Park elbowed him and wouldn't allow him in the door. I turned around and said to the bully, "Why don't you pick on someone your own size!"

"That's exactly what I want to do," he said, motioning his head toward the door.

We went out the door to the sidewalk. Five of his buddies were there and joined him.

Don Tangeman and Melvin Struthers came walking up the sidewalk from the lake right at that moment. I couldn't be-lieve my luck. The two happened to be home from college on vacation. They had been football tackles the year prior when we'd had our best football team ever.

Don was tall and slender but the strongest kid we ever knew. You couldn't tell by his appearance, but he was amazingly strong. I asked Don and Melvin if they'd stay and make sure the Arnolds Park guys would keep out of the fight. They agreed. It felt great to have Don backing me in case of trouble. He was both strong and fast. On a kick-off, he would often be in the other football team's backfield by the time the ball got there.

Don worked on a railroad repair crew during the summer months. An older guy once told me that two men would hold one end of a heavy rail, and Don would take care of the other end on his own.

There was a solid line of cars parked in front of the rink, so we walked into the street and started to fight. The bully and I knocked each other into the cars parked there. After some time, he'd had enough, and he walked away with his buddies. I came away with a black eye.

My eye was still bruised for the first basketball game. I told the coach my nephew had a yo-yo and hit me in the eye with it. I later heard that the football tackles told him a different story.

The Arnolds Park guys had graduated three years prior, and they all worked at the amusement park during the summers. At night, they would look for a guy walking alone. One of them would go up to him, elbow him, and start a fight. Then two or three more would join in until the poor guy was beat up, sometimes being pushed into an alley between the buildings.

I found out later that the parents of the bully who instigated the fight called my dad and complained. I don't know how they got my dad's name, what was said, or if they tried to get money from my dad. I do know that my dad drove down and talked to the parents.

When he got back home, Dad said to me, "If you think you look bad, you should see the other guy. Both his eyes are swollen shut, and he looks terrible!"

That's all my dad ever said to me on the subject.

Chapter 35

Shooting for
the Market

GRANDPA DAVE AND I STOOD in the middle of Jemmerson Slough atop a muskrat house. On this day, we didn't have the area to ourselves. Six hunters stood on the west end of the marshland. Grandpa and I spotted a white goose flying in our direction. Geese were uncommon to the area at the time. In all my years of hunting in Iowa before I moved away, I only saw a flock of geese fly overhead one time.

On the Christmas before I turned eleven, I'd received a break-action .410 shotgun as a gift. A 410 is named for its .41-inch bore diameter, a small bore compared to a 20-gauge or a 16-gauge. Most hunters have 12-gauge shotguns, but a .410 is great for new or young hunters because it's easy to handle and has little recoil.

The white goose flew directly over the group of men, but not one of them aimed at it. The bird wasn't flying high or anything—we figured the six hunters must have mistaken it for a seagull.

The bird flew toward Grandpa and me. Grandpa always let me shoot first, and if I missed, he'd kill it. I led the bird, pulled the trigger, and down came the goose. That was a big thrill of my young hunting days. It was my first goose, and at that point, I hadn't shot many ducks yet either.

That evening, we enjoyed a delicious goose dinner. Grandpa Dave and I picked the feathers off and cleaned the bird, and Grandma Maude and Aunt Fern prepared the meal.

GRANDPA DAVE SETTLED PERMANENTLY IN Spirit Lake back in 1907 when my dad was twelve years old. At the time, according to Grandpa, there were a large number of whistling swans out on Big Spirit Lake. People cooked and ate swans the same as they did geese. Whistling swans aren't as large as trumpeter swans, but they're bigger than geese. They had been a delicacy in the cities for a number of years. I never tasted a swan—by the time I was old enough to hunt, the swan population had dwindled in Iowa, and it became illegal to shoot them.

AREA HUNTERS SHOT DUCKS AND pheasants to feed their families. Skilled shooters such as my grandpa also shot for market. Shooting for market was a way for the best hunters to supplement their income. In Omaha, Chicago, Des Moines, and other cities, duck was a delicacy.

Shooting for the market wasn't for the average hunter. For most, it would be a pretty expensive endeavor, but champion shooters such as Dood Gilbert and Grandpa Dave didn't waste shells with poor aim. And they loaded their own shells to save money. After shooting, they'd search for and collect their empty shells in a bag. Before hunting again, they reloaded the shells with powder and lead shot. They also made connections and learned how and where to ship the birds.

My grandfather shot a lot of trap. They used to hold a big shoot every year in Terrill, Iowa. Grandpa won that competition, and I've got the trophy. Grandpa also won the state title two times.

On occasion, my grandpa would hitch two horses to a flatbed and drive west three miles on a moonlit night—from his farm to Grover's Lake. He'd tie up his horses, find a raised area, lie on his back, and wait for the mallards to fly overhead. Ducks were so plentiful that he could kill enough to fill the flatbed. Nice restaurants in the cities were always looking for ducks to purchase.

The same was true for fish. I remember a man from Omaha who sometimes came to Grandpa's boat livery. He'd go out on the lake with one of the guides to catch walleye. The man caught an abundance of walleyes. A guide who worked for Grandpa Dave cleaned them. A big freezer stood inside the entrance of the boat livery. Blocks of ice had been cut and placed inside the freezer. The guide stored the fish in the freezer once they were cleaned. When the man was ready to leave, Grandpa or one of the guides would chop ice from the block and fill a wooden box with walleyes and ice. The man delivered them two hundred miles away to a restaurant in Omaha.

Several years later when we were seining carp for the state, the state workers sold the seined carp to Stoller Fisheries. Stoller cleaned the carp and put the fish on ice. With their connections in Chicago, Stoller Fisheries sold the carp to street vendors. Ducks went to fancy restaurants, but carp sold well on the street—the city people were crazy for fish.

Chapter 36

Spirit Lake
Military Men

MY SISTER JEAN GRADUATED FROM high school in 1939. Every single boy in her graduating class joined the military or was drafted.

Jack Salliard, a classmate, was stationed in Sioux City, Iowa. Sioux City was about 120 miles from Spirit Lake by car. Jack was learning to fly a bomber, and the military offered flight training there. Jean and Irene knew him really well from school.

One day, Jack flew a plane from Sioux Falls to Spirit Lake. As he approached town, he flew very low—right above the treetops. He made a big circle, flew back over the town one more time, then headed back to Sioux City.

Many of the townspeople were shook up when it happened. Some even tried to get him kicked out of the service. Jack faced plenty of trouble, but it didn't last.

My sisters Jean and Irene thought the whole thing was exciting—they knew he was the kind of guy to do that sort of thing. All the young people thought it was the greatest thing that ever happened, but the older town folks thought they were being bombed by the Japanese or something. Jack went overseas and did his thing, I guess. I never did hear what happened to him.

....

BERKLEY BEDELL WAS ANOTHER HOMETOWN boy who flew bombers. Before the war started, my sister Jean worked for Berkley Bedell, making fishing tackle. When Berkley, who I mentioned in a previous chapter, was still in high school, he used his folks' car and went around selling fishing tackle. He started teaching women in town to tie flies.

Berkley would take the materials and drop them off at the women's homes, then return to pick up the flies and sell them to tackle shops in the area. In addition to teaching Berkley how to tie flies, Frank Marnett also taught him how to make leaders. Frank was the only one in the area who made anything like that at the time. A leader goes to the spinner. The line is heavy so it can be thrown, and the leader keeps the fish from spotting the line.

In 1942, Berkley joined the Army Air Corps. He learned how to fly those great big B-29 bombers, serving as a first lieutenant and flight instructor.

After Berkley came home from the war, leaders came to be a main Berkley Bedell product and biggest seller. He made millions because he worked hard and had good business sense.

The Spirit Lake governing body had traditionally opposed industry coming to town. But they allowed Berkley to build a business because he'd grown up in Spirit Lake, and his parents were both lawyers in town. Berkley's brother Jack eventually became a lawyer also, and my folks went to him. Jack bought the cottage that my friend JayDee Ferguson used to stay in during the summers. He and his wife fixed it up to be their regular home.

Berkley restarted his business after the war and did well. He built a multi-story brick factory in town. When he outgrew that, he built a huge factory on the other side of the cemetery, west of Spirit Lake. Business did so well that he opened a second factory in Emmetsburg, Iowa. It continued to grow, so he built a factory in Taiwan. One of his sons graduated with a degree and moved to Taiwan to run the business. Eventually, when Berkley retired, that son took over the company.

Originally, Berkley lived on Hill Street in a white house. I used to ride my bike past his house every day going to school. Later on, he bought a house down by the lake.

In addition to his tackle business, Berkley Bedell represented northwest Iowa in the U.S. Congress for twelve years. After I was out of college, he and his wife donated a parcel of land on the shores of East Okoboji. The eighty-acre Elinor Bedell State Park is named for his wife.

Chapter 37

Irene and Max Davis

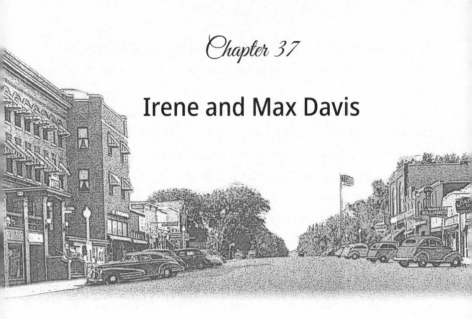

ONE DAY IRENE CAME HOME from school and said to me, "I bet I can make you blink."

She pretended like she was going to hit me in the face, but she accidentally forgot to stop her hand, and she socked me in the eye.

My sisters Jean and Irene didn't have much to do with me when we were growing up. I'm not sure why. Maybe the age difference was too great. They were nice to me when we were grown, though.

Irene married Max Davis when she was twenty years old. Max was quite a bit older. He had been born in Missouri and lived in Ottumwa, Iowa, where his parents ran the newspaper. Max wasn't the sort of guy who had experience with girls. He'd never dated a girl regularly before Irene. He told me that he just fell in love with my sister, and that was it.

Max earned a doctorate degree in biology. He worked for the State of Iowa, studying the life cycles of different types of fish. Back in those days, we didn't know that some fish could live one hundred years. Many fish live in a cycle, such as the silver bass. A five-year cycle. First, they hatch out. The second year, they're a little bit bigger. They're catchable with fly rods, but they might not be worth keeping because they're too small. The third year, they're almost grown. The fourth year, they're grown, and the fifth year, I don't know what happens to them. Max probably did. He studied the silver bass life cycle, but I never read his published results. I wish I had.

Max was truly a nice guy. He'd go hunting with other guys who worked for the state. When they walked along a ditch to hunt, there would be an abundance of tall reedy grasses to battle. The other guys walked on the edge of the ditch, but Max walked down the middle. The pheasants would fly out, and he'd let the other guys shoot them. He was willing to do the dirty work. He was just a great guy.

After Max and Irene were married, Max hoped to avoid being drafted. He enlisted in the Coast Guard, which was part of the Navy at the time. He was sent to San Diego to join his group for training, so he and Irene moved out there.

After their son Steve was born, Max was assigned to the USS Serpens, a crater-class cargo ship. The USS Serpens went into Guadalcanal, one of the Solomon Islands. The ship was loaded with all sorts of ammunition. They'd head to the location of the fleet and drop off ammunition to the ships that needed it. Then they'd return to Guadalcanal, fill up with ammunition, and run the mission all over again. The Coast Guard was similar to the Air Force in that after a man completed twenty-five missions, he was allowed to go home.

Max accomplished his twenty-five missions and was scheduled to return to the States. An officer hadn't been appointed to replace him, so Max volunteered for one more mission. When the ship reached Guadalcanal, the crew loaded the explosives. The ship's captain, first mate, and six crewmen were on shore. The rest were on the ship.

It was thought (but never proved) that a Japanese submarine snuck into the neck of the harbor and torpedoed the USS Serpens. Because the ship was full of ammunition, it blew up. One guy was blown out through a porthole, and one other survived. Two hundred fifty men died. The man blown through the porthole came to Spirit Lake to visit Irene one time. He had really been fond of Max.

Max volunteered for one extra mission, and he ended up paying for it with his life. The USS Serpens devastation in 1945 is the single greatest catastrophe in the history of the U.S. Coast Guard.[4]

A silver bass that Max caught and mounted hangs on the wall in my garage. Silver bass is also known as white bass. I used to have a mounted largemouth black bass from Max too, but that fell apart.

After Max was killed, Irene and Steve moved back to Spirit Lake and back into the folks' home. She didn't have any other place to go.

---

4. "USS Serpens Memorial," Arlington National Cemetery (website), retrieved May 26, 2023, https://www.arlingtoncemetery.mil/Explore/Monuments-and-Memorials/USS-Serpens.

Ensign Max Davis

The USS Serpens Memorial at Arlington National Cemetery
honors the U. S. Coast Guard members who died when the ship
exploded on January 29, 1945. The loss of the Serpens is the
largest single disaster ever suffered by the U.S. Coast Guard.

....

GLEN POWERS, AN ENGINEER FOR the Iowa Conservation Commission, supervised the building of the cement spillway between Mom's restaurant and Grandpa's boat livery. The cement spillway replaced the long-time dirt spillway between Big Spirit Lake and East Okoboji.

Glen and another guy were out on the shore one day, horsing around, throwing stuff up, and shooting at it. Glen used a 16-gauge automatic. Most hunters had 12-gauge and 20-gauge shotguns, but he owned a 16-gauge. My aunt Fern had one too. It's in-between sizes and doesn't kick as much.

That's when he and Irene met.

Glen started to talk with Irene frequently, and they began spending time together. In 1947, they married and built a cottage next to the folks. They added three children to their family. Glen eventually became director of the Iowa Conservation Department. Later, their family moved to Indianola, Iowa, where Glen worked for the city. In the 1970s, they retired to Tucumcari, New Mexico.

Chapter 38

Jean and George Dawson

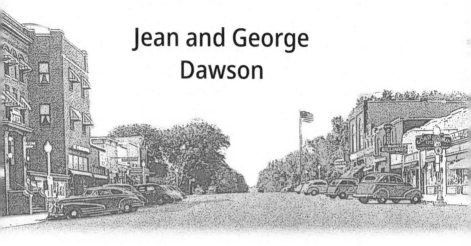

MY SECOND OLDEST SISTER'S GIVEN name was Ormagene. Throughout her years in school, it's the name her teachers and classmates used. She never cared for it. She preferred Jean, which is what our family always called her.

My sister Jean attended beauty school in Sioux City. Afterward, she worked in salons, first in Milford and then in Spirit Lake. The shop in Spirit Lake was one of two competing salons, both situated directly above the town barbershop.

In 1942, my sister Jean and a friend traveled to California, hoping to get jobs at the defense plant there. The other girl was from Arnolds Park—her dad was in politics. Both Jean and her friend were hired. Irene was also in the area because her husband was stationed there.

A young man named George Dawson worked in the same defense plant. Jean told Irene that George was the best-looking guy she'd ever seen. She said she was interested in him because he was a nice guy, but his looks were an added bonus.

Jean and George started dating a few months after she moved to San Diego. In 1943, after an eleven-month courtship, they were married. George was drafted into the Army, and Jean returned to Iowa to live with her folks. He only received a few weeks of military training, and then he was assigned to a ship. The military needed a large number of servicemen for the big D-Day invasion.

George escaped injury on D-Day. But afterward, his unit was on night patrol, and he was shot and seriously wounded by a German sniper. The bullet hit him in the front and went clear through his body. Medical personnel worked on him, then sent him back to the States to recover.

Jean and George had lived on Coronado Island before George was drafted. After the war, they settled in San Diego and raised their two daughters, Dianne and Barbara, there. George worked on jet planes on Coronado Island until his retirement.

Chapter 39

Seeds of Faith

G RANDPA DAVE WAS RAISED A Baptist. His father had been a Baptist minister in Sweden. When the family moved to the United States, they started near Village Creek, Iowa, because friends lived there.

The family learned of opportunities to homestead in South Dakota, so they moved to the Big Springs area and began to farm. Down the road less than a mile was a Baptist church without a preacher. So, Grandpa Dave's father gave the message on Sundays. Whenever there was a wedding or funeral, he took care of it. However, he had a large and growing family, and he couldn't earn enough to live on as a preacher. So, during the week, he farmed and earned most of his living by farming.

When I stopped by that church many years later, a picture of Grandpa Dave's father hung in the building, and his name was spelled Nilson. On his tombstone in the churchyard was carved: Carl J. Nilson. Christine C. Nilson was on his wife's stone.

I'm not sure when the spelling of the family name changed from Nilson to Nelson. One of Grandpa's older brothers, Joel, owned a hotel. When he started doing business, it's likely he changed the name from Nilson to Nelson to sound more American.

When Grandpa Dave moved to Spirit Lake, there wasn't a Baptist church in town, so he attended the Presbyterian church. I'm not sure what protestant church Grandma Maude was raised in. I know her father came from Lincolnshire, England, and she came to faith in Christ as a young girl. I'm not sure if she attended a different church in town or not. Nobody ever told me much, and I didn't ask.

I was very fond of Grandpa Dave. On Sundays, I would ride my bike or walk on my own to the Presbyterian church. I attended Sunday school in the basement, then sat with my grandpa during the church service.

In junior high, I started going to the Methodist church. Tommy Carver, Jim Norman, and other guys I ran around with attended the Methodist church with their families, and I wanted to be with my friends.

My friends and I joined a confirmation program where we learned about becoming members of the church. We went through the program together. Around the time we moved from junior high to high school, we completed the program, and I was baptized and joined the church.

....

I NEVER GOT TO KNOW my maternal grandpa, John T. Baker. He made a living with cattle. Before he retired, my grandparents bought a farm for each of their four living sons and their oldest daughter. Unfortunately, my mother was the second youngest of their eleven children. Since she was a girl, she and my dad never received financial help. Grandpa Baker died when I was five years old.

When my folks took me a few times to Grandma and Grandpa Baker's farmhouse, Grandpa was never there. He was always out checking on his cattle or one of his kids' farms. Still, we'd visit with Grandma. She had a pantry in her kitchen, and I thought it was the greatest thing. The shelves were filled with jars of vegetables, meat, and fruit she had canned, but the best part was the cookie jar.

On the other side of the house, a long hallway led to the bedrooms. Along the wall on both sides hung thirteen framed oval photos, individually featuring my grandparents and their eleven children. I was only four or five, but I loved looking at the huge family pictures.

When Grandma Minnie took a small apartment at the Marion Hotel and I would stop to see her, she enjoyed talking about life and cooking and the Bible. She told me she read her leather-bound Bible every day. I sometimes caught her in the act. She liked to share with me what she was reading and often quoted some of her favorite verses.

....

WHEN WE LIVED ON THE farm, I sometimes saw my folks reading our family Bible. Most area families owned a large family Bible. They kept records of births, marriages, and deaths in the front pages.

Even though my folks read the Bible, they only took us to church twice, that I can remember. Both times were on Easter Sunday. I always assumed the reason they didn't go to church every Sunday while we were on the farm was because they didn't have money to give. Cash was hard to come by, and I doubt they'd have felt comfortable attending without contributing when the plate was passed. Nobody ever told me, but that's what I always thought.

Chapter 40

Spirit Lake Schools

IN MY YOUNGER YEARS, WE said the Pledge of Allegiance in many of our classes at the start of each school day. The rules at school were:

1. No throwing
2. No gum
3. No beanshooters[5]

Students who did something wrong were required to stay after school and listen to a lecture from the teacher. Jim Norman and I had to stay after once when we were in third grade. I can't remember the offense.

Nobody ever swore in school, even in junior high or high school. Even in the locker rooms after sports practice.

In junior high, which was sixth, seventh, and eighth grades, all students reported to the assembly hall at the beginning of the day. Each student had their own assigned desk

---

5. An inflexible tube through which dried beans or peas are blown.

in the assembly hall. Sixth-grade desks were on one side, seventh-grade desks in the middle, and eighth-grade desks on the opposite side. Our female principal's desk was at the front of the room.

Students went to separate rooms for each class. There were chairs with a swivel tablet surface for students in each room. We had a different teacher for each subject.

Our principal was the best English teacher I had in my life, including high school and college. She taught it all to us. I'm afraid it didn't all sink in, but she taught it to us.

Mr. Means was a favorite teacher. He was a younger guy who taught civics. He kept our interest, so we actually paid attention to what he taught. He also shared his personal life with us. We heard about his V8 Ford engine and learned about driving. He told us that if the lights of an oncoming car were blinding at night, it helped to focus on the white line at the edge of the road. That advice has been a lifesaver for me.

One year, he was also our basketball coach. He and his wife lived in an apartment in town. My friends and I stopped by his place one time.

Mr. Means taught gym class too. Boxing matches were popular then, and he liked to have the boys box each other. Because of my boxing experience, I kept my nose out of that. As I said before, I don't think anyone at school ever knew I boxed. Jim Norman was good-sized and left-handed. When we were in seventh grade, he won all his matches against the seventh- and eighth-grade boys.

In high school, every student had a desk in the assembly hall, just like in junior high. The principal's desk stood on a platform in front of the room. Seniors were on the left, then juniors, then sophomores, with freshmen on the right side of the room. Students walked to individual rooms for each subject and sat in chairs. We brought a notepad and book with us to class.

All students were scheduled two forty-five-minute study periods each day in the assembly hall. That's when I got my homework done every day. In thirteen years of school, I never took a book home.

The worst thing that ever happened in all my years of school happened during a high school study period. For all study periods, there was always a teacher in charge who sat at the principal's desk. The teacher could see all the students at their desks from that vantage point.

A freshman girl near the back of the study hall raised her hand, and the male teacher shook his head, indicating no. Students normally raised a hand if they wanted permission to use the restroom. After several minutes passed, she raised her hand again, and the teacher looked displeased and shook his head no again. A short time later, the girl wet her pants and ran to the front of the study hall and right down the hallway to the restrooms.

That was the most disrespectful thing done by a teacher I had ever seen in my life. I would have given my summer's wages to spend ten minutes in the boxing ring with him. I couldn't imagine how ashamed and terrible that poor girl must have felt. I think one of the female teachers helped her out and comforted her.

I still get tears in my eyes thinking about that poor freshman girl. To make a young girl endure that experience in front of the entire high school and then have to return to class was terrible. If I were her, I wouldn't have been able to handle it.

....

SPIRIT LAKE OFFERED FOOTBALL, BASKETBALL, and track after school for boys, and I was involved in all three. I was passionate about sports, but because I wanted to go to college, I did my best to do well in my classes also. I was one of two boys in my class elected to the honor society. Besides sports, I participated in two school plays while in high school. My parents never attended the plays—nor even one of my games. The restaurant was a priority for them.

Jerry and Lorna and their boys, Bob and Dick, came to one football game my senior year when we played in Storm Lake. Jerry was a game warden south of there at the time. I played end on offense. I dove and caught a long pass during that game and kept it off the ground, but the referee happened to be on the far end of the field, and he called it incomplete.

Grandpa Dave and Aunt Fern came to quite a few of our home basketball games during the three years I was on the starting five. I wish my parents would have come to something, but they were always busy with the restaurant.

Chapter 41

Dances at the Library

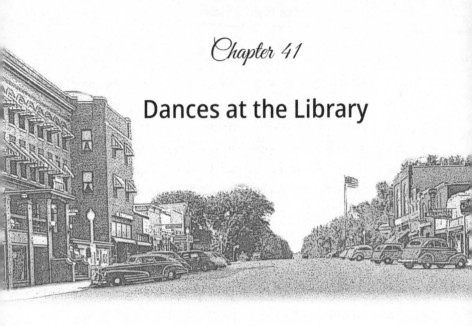

MY GOOD FRIEND TOMMY CARVER wasn't timid at all around girls, but I was incredibly shy. I envied his ability to talk with girls and be comfortable around them.

One time when we were in sixth grade, Tom made arrangements with a girl and two of her friends. Jim Norman, Tommy, and I were excited to have a date to the movies with three sixth-grade girls, thanks to Tommy's outgoing nature. I enjoyed my time, but I was careful with my money. I focused on saving for college and didn't go on a date again for a long time.

When we were in seventh grade, a few of the girls in our class with recreation rooms in their basements would invite the boys and girls from school to come and dance on a Friday or Saturday night. I could dance, but I don't remember how I learned.

In seventh grade, Jim Norman learned it was possible to rent the library basement. The Spirit Lake Public Library was located at 1801 Hill Avenue, down the street from the school.

It was a single-story brick building built on a raised basement. Jim, Tommy, and I decided to rent the basement and host a Saturday night dance.

The three of us invited all the kids we knew well. To earn enough to pay the library rental fee, we charged each person an admission fee of fifty cents. Tommy brought his record player and records. He owned a lot of records. Everyone came on their own and left on their own. There were no couples or dates.

The dance was such a success that we continued hosting them for quite a few Saturdays during our seventh- and eighth-grade years. The dances gave kids who were interested in socializing an inexpensive place to go. Jim, Tommy, and I kept things simple. We didn't decorate or serve any food or drinks, but kids came anyway. And there wasn't much clean up.

Spirit Lake Carnegie Library, 1801 Hill Avenue

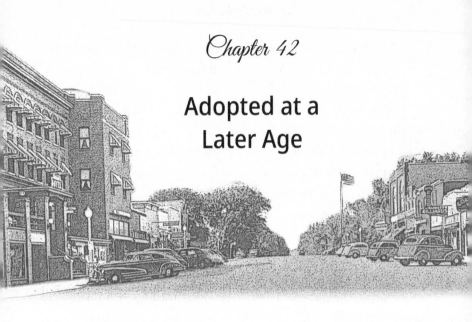

Chapter 42

Adopted at a Later Age

MANY IN MY CLASS STARTED school in kindergarten and continued together all the way through high school graduation. A couple of students joined our class later after being adopted by older couples in the community who wanted an older child.

Robert (Bob) Schneidawind came to us at the start of eighth grade. He was the tallest kid in our class. Bob was six feet, nine inches by the time we were high school seniors. Because of his height, he started as center on our junior high basketball team.

Dave Dean, our other tall kid, moved over to play forward. I was the starting guard in seventh and eighth grades, and our team was undefeated both years.

Joe Schneidawind was the town blacksmith. His home and shop were located in the northeast part of Spirit Lake. His wife was from the Arp family, who owned the biggest grocery store in Spirit Lake. The couple adopted Bob from Father Flanagan's Boys Home, also known as Boys Town, in Nebraska.[6]

The Schneidawinds had an acreage with their home and owned a cow. Bob needed to milk the cow every day when he got home from school. Bob played end on our football team during his junior and senior years. He was a really nice guy and a good athlete.

Virginia Moeller joined our class when we were in sixth grade. Her parents were older and wanted a child. Virginia's birth parents had more children than they could afford to raise, so they found it necessary to adopt some out.

Virginia was a blonde of "normal" height and weight. That was the only thing normal about her—in a good way. She took part in just about everything our school had to offer. She was a cheerleader in junior high and senior high.

My mother had a friend who gave tap dancing lessons, so she signed me up. The studio was next to the movie theater in Spirit Lake. I did not want to learn tap dancing, and the class was all girls except for me. After several lessons, I quit.

Virginia turned out to be a wonderful dancer. Her parents probably paid dearly for her to get to that point. She was the best dancer of all the high school girls, and she could follow anyone no matter how clumsy we were. Three girls and two boys made the Honor Society. I was one of the boys, and Virginia was one of the girls.

A jitterbug contest was held in Spirit Lake, and I asked Virginia to be my partner. We practiced a couple of times and ended up winning the contest, mainly due to Virginia. When we were seniors, I was the football captain, and Virginia was

---

6. www.boystown.org

the homecoming queen. We had our picture taken together in the middle of the football field.

Virginia must have been double-jointed or something. When we were sophomores, a teacher talked her into putting on a show for the school. The show was held in the school auditorium, and all classes attended. She could wrap both legs around her neck. She did that once and rolled across the stage like a ball. She did all manner of twists and turns with her body that none of the rest of us could possibly do. I don't remember the details of the whole show, but it was amazing.

While she was in high school, Virginia's dad died, and then when she was starting her senior year, her mother died too. The school principal and his wife took Virginia in to live with them for the rest of the school year.

Jim Norman, a good friend of mine, had been dating Virginia at the time. Jim's dad ran the Ford garage in town. After Virginia's mother died, the principal said there would be no more dating for the rest of the year.

I lost track of Virginia after graduation, but I heard she went to college and married a man from Milford. Her picture was in the paper once. She was riding a fine-looking horse on their property.

Chapter 43

Spirit Lake Athletics

I N SIXTH GRADE, BOYS INTERESTED in football were taught how to block and tackle. The coach handed down old high school uniforms to us. The coach's son was on the high school team, and he showed us how to drop-kick the football.

In seventh grade, I went out for basketball and beat an eighth-grade student to be a starting guard. We won all our junior high games that year. In eighth grade, I was able to start every game, and we were undefeated for the second year in a row.

My freshman year, I had high hopes of playing basketball on the second team, but my hopes were dashed. The second team was mainly freshmen and sophomores, but the coach included some juniors who didn't get much playing time with the first team. I only got to play for twenty seconds at the end of one game that season. I didn't go out for football that year since I only weighed 125 or 130 pounds. And I didn't even bother trying out for track because I didn't think I could run fast enough.

I tried out for football my sophomore year. The last week of practice, I beat out the senior who had initially been picked for starting left guard. I weighed about 135 pounds and was the lightest guy on the team, but I was quick and strong for my size. If a back came through on my side of the line, he got tackled. I always tackled as low as I could. Some big fullbacks would drag me a yard or two, but I never let go.

We had a good team but a terrible quarterback. He never completed a pass the entire season, and he was also poor at calling plays. The coach said he chose him because he was good at math, but we all knew he was a relative of the coach's wife. One of our halfbacks managed to complete several passes for us. We probably won about half our games that season. We were the smallest town and the smallest school in our eight-team conference.

I tried out for basketball again. This time, the coach put me on the first team, but I had no idea why. I never practiced with the starting five, but the night of our first game, in the locker room, the coach said, "Nelson, start at forward."

That was a shock. I made some long shots that game, so he kept me on the starting five. We won about half our games for the year.

I didn't go out for track, but I walked out after school one day and watched the track team practice for a bit. Four guys were practicing pole vaulting. After watching for a while, I asked if I could try. Only one of the guys could clear nine feet, so after I cleared nine feet, then nine and a half feet, I asked the coach if I could join the track team.

I became the main pole vaulter after that. I high-jumped too. We used aluminum poles for vaulting at the time. They had no flex or give at all. In college, we used bamboo poles, which were a little more flexible.

As I stood with the coach one time, a teammate came up and asked the coach why I was so good at pole vaulting. Our coach, John T. Webb, said, "That's because Neil rows so much."

The coach probably knew my grandpa owned a boat livery. I was out on the lake rowing all the time. I worked as a guide for Grandpa Dave now and then too. Guides took tourists out on the lake for the day and gave guidance on where to fish. I never thought about it at the time, but I guess the rowing was good exercise.

The summer before my junior year, I worked with the State of Iowa dynamite crew. We blew ditches between two lakes. We waded in mud through sloughs all summer.

After working so hard, I was in great shape for football when practice started. I played center on offense and linebacker on defense. We played a single wing.

All four backfielders stood some distance back, so I had to hike the ball to the player who would run or pass the ball. It wasn't like the T-formation of today, where the quarterback stands behind the center and gets the ball. I don't think I ever missed a tackle on my side of the line while playing defense. I enjoyed basketball and track, but I loved football.

We ended up having the best team in Spirit Lake's history. Cherokee beat us, so we came in second in our conference. We were the only team to score on Cherokee. We made two or three touchdowns. I think they scored four on us. We beat Estherville 25 to 6. The coach said Spirit Lake hadn't beaten Estherville in over twenty years. Estherville had two meat packing plants and plenty of big, tough kids on their team.

Cherokee was voted the top football team in the State of Iowa for the year.

My junior year, our team beat Spencer. It was one of the big thrills of my life. Spencer was the largest town in the conference, with the largest student population. We played at Spencer that year. I weighed 150 pounds. For the three weeks before we played Spencer, our guys were saying that no one could beat this team, which had a senior who had been first-team all-state tackle the year prior. To make two to four yards each play, Spencer just had to follow this tackle.

On the opening kick-off, I was running downfield at full speed when I saw a really big guy straight ahead of me. When I got a couple of yards from him, I turned sideways and hit him in the stomach with my side. I may have had rib pads on. They carried him off the field, and he didn't come back out for the entire game. I know from experience that when you have the air knocked out of you, it feels as if you're dying. Since their all-state tackle was in for only the first play of the game, we ended up winning 7 to 6.

My senior year, I was selected as captain of the football team. Near the end of the school year, I was offered a full scholarship to attend the University of Iowa in Iowa City. I had suffered two concussions, cracked ribs, and I had an issue with weak ankles. Even though I loved the idea of winning a scholarship and playing football, I wanted to be an engineer. I decided to focus on academics in college, and I turned the scholarship down.

Football Program

AND SCORE CARD

Friday, October 3, 1947

EMMETSBURG E'HAWKS

vs.

SPIRIT LAKE INDIANS

	1	2	3	4	Final

STARTING LINE-UPS

	SPIRIT LAKE			EMMETSBURG	
Numbers	Names	Positions		Names	Numbers
29	NEIL NELSON (Capt.)	L. E.		JERRY JONDAHL	28
43	EVERETT BAKER	L. T.		BILL GOWAN	38
26	KENNETH REED	L. G.		TED GRAVES	26
22	BRUCE CHENEY	C.		DALE OHRTMAN	32
28	BERNARD COHRS	R. G.		DON QUAM	30
44	DAVID DEAN	R. T.		PHIL STILLMAN	35
31	BOB SCHNEIDAWIND	R. E.		ALAN FROST	39
32	CHARLES HEICK	I. B.		DALE FORDYCE	22
33	DUANE YAGER	L. H.		JOE DIRKX	25
34	MERLIN HEIDT	R. H.		RUSSELL HITE	24
35	BOB BAIN	F B.		GORDON NICHOLS	23

RESERVES

37	BOB JECK	C.		BILL PITCHER	34
38	BILL RODAWIG	C.			
23	HARRY SMITH	G.		CHUCK SPIES	29
27	GEORGE STARR	G.		FRINK	31
33	IREL BRUNS	G.			
51	MERLYN STRUTHERS	G.			
54	DICK MARNELL	G.			
36	MELVIN FROENDT	T.		KORLASKE	36
40	BILL MC CLINTIC	T.		NAIG	27
25	ED SWANSON	T.		SCHUMACKER	41
39	KENNETH SWANSON	T.			
24	BOB TANGEMAN	E.		J. FROST	37
42	JACK MALMGREN	E.		WALKER	42
	BOB WORKHOVEN	E.			
	DON AHRENS	E.			
41	L. (Bud) Waugh	Back		JOHNNY PAPADAKES	33
21	DON BOEHM	Back		VAUGHAN	21
52	DICK DEAN	Back		KINNETZ	20
20	BOB WAUGH	Back		L. PAPADAKES	
30	MARVIN JONES	Back			

COACHES: John Webb - Leon Uknes   COACH: Edward Cisler

Officials: M. O. Moe, Lake Park - C. W. Felt, Spencer - Jake Hoekstra, Ruthven
NEXT HOME GAME - SIBLEY - OCTOBER 24

143

....

WE HAD A GOOD BASKETBALL team that year, but Spencer was better, and their center, Kenny DeCoster, made the all-state first team. We weren't a high-scoring team—we played slowly and deliberately. Most of the teams in our conference were similar, but Spencer was more upbeat. They beat us 46 to 36 in one of our games.

Lake Park had the best basketball team they'd ever had that year. The son of the town dentist was six feet, eight inches tall, and played center. A six-foot-two forward moved to Lake Park, and he was really good at basketball. Their guard was a good player, and his younger brother played for the next two years. He was even better. Lake Park was winning all their games by a big margin. Their coach thought they were special, but he really didn't know how good they were.

He called our coach almost every day, wanting to play a game against Spirit Lake. Our coach couldn't schedule extra games, but he finally gave in and said they could come over and scrimmage our team. The coaches found a couple of volunteer referees.

We played our game against Lake Park with no audience. It ended 50 to 25. Lake Park had 25. Since they were a smaller school, they weren't used to the caliber of teams we played against. Our center was also six feet, eight inches, which probably made a difference too.

Our biggest game was early in the season against South Sioux City. We were a warm-up game before their season schedule. The year before, they were in the final game of the state tournament, and they lost. Now they had several returning players and were highly rated in the state.

We played at Spirit Lake. The South Sioux City players kept taunting us, saying things such as, "What do you hayseeds eat up here anyway?"

They continued their insults throughout the game. We won 34 to 32, and it was the highlight of our playing days.

Nimrod was their six-foot-two or six-foot-three forward and the best player on their team. Later in track that year, at the district track meet, I beat him and also Holsclaw from Estherville, who was rated the best pole vaulter in the state. I was the first athlete from Spirit Lake to ever compete in the state track meet in Des Moines.

I met and got to know Nimrod later at Boys State, a civics and leadership training program for high school students. I found out that Nimrod was a good guy, and it turned out I really liked him.

1946–47 varsity football starters (from left, front row): Bob Schneidawind, Don Tangeman, Bob Bains, Neil Nelson, Kenneth Reid, Melvin Struthers, Kenneth Bunce (back row) Delbert Bryan, Red Griffith, Bob Thoelke, Bud Houchins

1947–48 varsity basketball team (from left, front row): Merlin Heidt, Tom Carver, Jim Norman; (second row) Bob Jeck, Duane Yager, Bill Norman, Neil Nelson, Lionel "Bud" Waugh; (back row) David Dean, Dick Dean, Bruce Cheney, Bob Schneidawind, Harry "Dud" Smith

Chapter 44

Advertising for
a Spouse

THREE OF MY SCHOOL FRIENDS moved to the area as a result of their mothers corresponding with men from Spirit Lake. In each case, the correspondence led to marriage.

Harry Dudley Smith became a great friend of mine. Everyone called him Dud. He had lived in Little Rock, Arkansas, with his mother and moved to Spirit Lake the year before we started kindergarten.

Harry's mom moved from Arkansas because Jack Boehm had advertised for a nanny. Harry's mom took care of Jack Boehm's kids and kept house for him for a couple of years. She and Dud lived in separate quarters until Jack Boehm and Dud's mom were married.

Turp, one of the younger Boehm kids, was a terrific boxer with the fastest reflexes of anyone I ever saw. He probably would've hit me twice when I hit him once. His reflexes were unbelievable. He made it to the Golden Gloves in Chicago.

That's probably the only time he got beat. I heard that in Chicago, he looked up at his girlfriend, and the distraction cost him the match.

The youngest Boehm boy joined the paratroopers. He told Harry and me that he could earn fifty dollars a month more. I told Harry that I wouldn't jump out of a plane to make *five hundred* dollars more a month.

Harry Smith and I were on Hill Avenue after school one day. As we walked along on the sidewalk, when we got to the pool hall, there was no pool hall there anymore. Harry and I had no idea there had been a fire, but we must have missed a big one. The roof and the sides of the building were burned up, and everything had fallen down into the basement.

As we peered over the edge, we could see coins down there. Lots of nickels and pennies. We wished we could reach down and get the money. It never dawned on us that the change belonged to Bill Barrett, the pool hall owner.

Bill must have had good insurance because he rebuilt the whole place.

Later in high school, Harry and I were on the track team together. Harry ran on the two-mile relay team with Tommy Carver. It was a terrific relay team.

....

RON BOOTHE CAME TO SPIRIT Lake when we were in high school. An electrician in Spirit Lake had advertised in the Des Moines Register. Ron and his mother moved up from Des Moines, and I think his mom married the electrician when she arrived. Ron said he had been in a gang in Des Moines. I don't think he ever got close to anyone in high school. I used to see him at Arnolds Park when I went there.

Ron was fairly tall and had dark hair. It was general knowledge that the girls at Arnolds Park thought he was handsome.

He wore a light jacket and always wore his collar turned up. I don't think he ever dated any of the local Spirit Lake girls.

Ron ran on our two-mile relay team with Tommy and Harry. After high school, Ron went to Estherville Junior College for two years. A couple from Estherville and their daughters used to come into Mom's restaurant. They owned a nearby cottage on Spirit Lake. Ron married one of the daughters and found a job in Sioux City, Iowa.

....

DON AHRENS JOINED OUR CLASS when we were in high school too. His mother answered an ad in the Sioux City paper. She came to Spirit Lake and married a man named E. C. Weaver. Don's stepfather was the oldest of three siblings. He and his brothers seined minnows from the Little Sioux River.

The Weaver brothers had a truck with a water tank on the back full of minnows. The tank had a pump to supply air to them. They sold minnows to the boat liveries around Spirit Lake, East Okoboji Lake, and West Okoboji Lake.

My grandfather had a large tank between his boathouse and the lake. The Weaver brothers would dip out minnows and place them in his tank. The Weavers sold minnows by the type and by the dozen. Grandpa kept water from the lake in the tank and a pump running air into it.

Later, Mr. Weaver bought a boat livery on the west side of West Okoboji Lake. He called it Weaver's Boat Livery. It was the only boat livery on that side of the lake. The two other brothers continued with the minnow business.

Don ran on the relay team with Tommy, Harry, and Ron. He liked to hunt and fish too. He worked for a business in Arnolds Park after he graduated from school and lived in Okoboji.

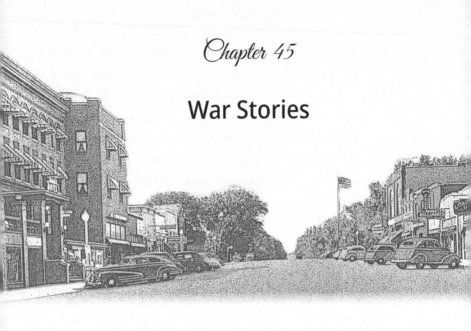

Chapter 45

War Stories

J UNIOR FRONK, PEARL FRONK'S SON, used to stop at Mom's café, order coffee, and talk to us. I would sit at the counter next to Junior and Mom pulled up a chair on the other side when she wasn't busy. Pearl worked for Grandpa Dave as a fishing guide at the Orleans Boat Livery for many years. I always liked Pearl. He was a slim man, and his son Junior was too. And Junior wasn't tall either. He didn't look like a guy who would become a war hero.

Junior was several years older than me. He didn't go out for sports or extracurriculars, but he was a really nice kid. He was a meek, shy guy, but during his high school years, shortly before the war, he began stopping by the restaurant. Junior would order a cup of coffee and talk to Mom and me. We enjoyed our conversations with him.

When the war came, Junior enlisted in the Army. He made it into the Army Rangers—he actually became one of the original Darby's Rangers. Junior served in the 1st and the

4th Ranger Battalions. Unlike many of the Rangers, Junior survived the war and returned home in May 1944. He stopped by the restaurant, and we could barely believe he was the same young man. He looked very well-built.

> Darby's Rangers were specialized American troops, rigorously trained by British commandos. Colonel William O. Darby was a military officer known for his leadership skills.[7]

Junior told me about his time in the Pacific. If the Allies planned to attack an island, his small unit would be taken by submarine close to shore. The Army Rangers would sneak onto the island in rubber rafts. Their task was to destroy gasoline dumps and oil dumps and to knock out enemy communications. The Rangers were given a deadline and were expected to accomplish their tasks in short order.

Junior and the other Rangers approached these islands in enemy territory. They were provided the location to board the nearby sub after their mission, and that was the only support they had.

Darby's Rangers were in enemy territory without any backup. Under cover of darkness, the men needed to paddle back out to board the submarine and escape. Junior did that during the Pacific campaign.

After he was discharged, Junior talked with me at the restaurant for a long time. He asked me to go into the back room with him to show me something. In the back room, he

---

7. "Ranger William O. Darby," Descendants of WWII Rangers, INC (website), retrieved May 26, 2023, https://wwiirangers.org/our-rangers/william-o-darby-2/.

removed his clothing except his shorts. His entire body showed evidence of being hit by flak.

When the war ended, Junior Fronk wasn't called Junior anymore. Everyone called him Rocky. He had always been a super nice kid, and I can't begin to imagine all he went through.

....

MY COUSIN WAYNE FRONK SERVED in the Navy during the war. He was stationed in New Guinea, tasked with building airfields and roads. Locals worked side by side with servicemen. Day after day, pilots of single-seat Japanese Zeroes would fly over and strafe them. Wayne told me that some of the guys on the ground couldn't handle the pressure.

One of the young locals ran around, out of his mind, after the strafing. They'd dug ditches the men used for a bathroom. The guy ran over and dove into one of those latrines. It's hard to imagine the stress of the Japanese attacking from low-flying aircraft day after day.

....

WHEN MY COUSIN WAYNE WAS in his eighties and his wife had died, he moved back to Spirit Lake from California. He faced vision issues, and they progressed so that he could hardly see. His son was unable to help him, due to health reasons, so Rocky took over. Wayne and Rocky were cousins. He helped Wayne get situated in a little house in Spirit Lake where he could live close to the grocery store. Not only was Rocky a war hero, he was a good guy.

T/SGT Junior "Rocky" Fronk

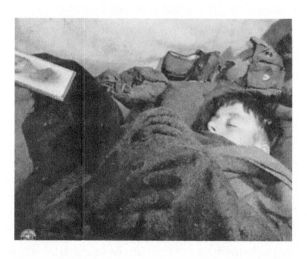

Rocky training with the British Commando Forces in Scotland. Taking a nap while a picture of Mom watches over him (US Signal Corps picture).

Chapter 46

Model A

I BOUGHT A 1930 MODEL A car for 150 dollars after I turned sixteen and passed the driver's test. My dad helped me through the car-buying process. I went to an insurance agent's office downtown and bought insurance. The law required drivers to have their registration in a holder with a cellophane window mounted on the steering column in case of a stop by the police. The registration needed to be in view for the police officer to see. Thin springs held the holder in place.

When I needed tires for the car, I bought recaps. Tires were not available for sale at all during World War II. People in Spirit Lake could buy retread, but not new tires. Drivers took old tires and put retread around them. Some people in cities were able to purchase tires on the black market, but I had no idea how the black market worked.

When I purchased my used Model A, I wasn't the greatest driver. I drove too fast. The highway that went past the restaurant and the folks' cottage turned ninety degrees near the pump station. After the turn, there was a railroad track, and then it was a straight shot toward Spirit Lake.

One day I came around the corner too fast, and my car slid down onto the railroad track across from our cottage near where the fish hatchery was. I landed with my wheels straddling the track, and the track was up fairly high from the ground. I couldn't believe how stupid I had been. I was scared to death that I was going to have to leave my car, but I fiddled around for a good half hour and finally got the car out of there and back on the road. That was the worst thing I ever remember doing.

Once when I went to a movie, I parked my Model A across the street from the theater. I went alone, so after the movies, I got into my car. It must have been a Saturday afternoon because it was light out. I drove south about a quarter of a block and turned west on Highway 9, then turned right and went north two blocks. I turned east in front of the electrical power station, where I should have but didn't slow up for the corner.

All at once, the driver's side rear dropped down, and I saw my rear tire flying by. The tire rolled half a block, crossed the sidewalk on the left side of the street, then proceeded to roll into the back door of the hotel where we used to live.

It took every tool I owned and a lot of time to get the axle raised and the wheel back on. I was able to find most of the nuts to secure the tire rim.

I found out later that Tommy Carver and a few buddies had loosened all the nuts on that back rim and tire.

A couple of weeks later, Tommy Carver parked his Model T car on the same side of the street as mine had been, only further north down the block. I looked around for a while and couldn't locate him, so I found four other guys in town to help me. We pushed Tommy's car up on the sidewalk and south a bit. We left it on the sidewalk right in front of Bill Barrett's pool hall. I never heard out how Tommy got his car off the sidewalk, but I'm sure he knew who instigated the prank.

Chapter 47

A Trip Down the
Des Moines River

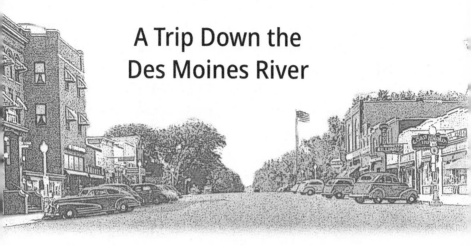

MAX SHEPARD AND I TOOK a weeklong boat trip down the Des Moines River. We traveled from Estherville, Iowa, to Rutland, where there is a dam in the river. Somehow, I was able to get a week off work to make the trip. That was a big deal. It never happened any other summer.

A fisherman in need of cash had sold his light plywood boat to my grandfather for twenty-five dollars. Grandpa let me have the boat for what he paid. I bought an old pair of oars and cut them down for the smaller boat. After shaping them, I secured the hardware with leather rings and loops that fit into the boat.

We used my boat and Max's tent and camping equipment. We brought food along to start our trip, and we bought cans of Spam, which we fried. I had never eaten Spam before—we thought it tasted good.

Red Daniels was the son of Bud Daniels, a guide at Grandpa's boat livery. Bud's wife often worked as a waitress for my mom whenever she needed extra help at the restaurant. Red made his living delivering gravel in his truck. He hauled the boat, the camping equipment, Max, and me to a park near the Des Moines River in Estherville. We unloaded everything and started our journey from there.

Max worked for the state at the fish hatchery. He was several years older than I. His father Seth had worked there too, and their family lived across the gravel road from the fish hatchery.

Max enjoyed the outdoors. He ran a trap line every winter for muskrats and mink. He liked to hunt ducks in the sloughs close to Big Spirit Lake, and he did a lot of fishing. Max and I went fishing together several times before our trip.

We didn't go far the first day. We set up camp and put up our tent in a farmer's pasture along the river just past Wallingford. Max collected wood for the fire, and we made a little pit for the wood. He'd brought along a small skillet for frying Spam and fish.

We found a couple of willow sticks and added a fishing line with a hook and sinker to each. I caught a frog and cut it in two for bait. We pushed the large end of each stick into the bank of the river. These were called diddly poles. With diddly poles, when a catfish strikes the frog, the willow bends and sets the hook.

Later one night, we caught two blue catfish. They were about six pounds each. I didn't know about blue catfish but found out they are better tasting than regular black catfish. After eating, we cleaned everything in the sand along the river. We never used soap and water the entire trip, so that was a new experience for me.

Max and I went by Graettinger the next day, and we also passed the highway leading into Emmetsburg. We stopped and walked into town to pick up a few groceries. In the store, the shopkeeper informed us that the United States had used an airplane to drop a new type of bomb—an atomic bomb—on Japan. The date was Monday, August 6, 1945, and I was fifteen years old. I have always remembered where I was when I heard that news.

Soon afterward, we started to search downriver for a suitable campsite. We chose a spot near a pasture along the river again. As Max collected firewood and chopped some with his hatchet, he accidentally cut into one of his knees. We'd brought along a small first aid kit, so we used what we had to patch his wound. He kept it covered for the rest of the trip.

Along the way, we caught fish but only kept the larger ones to eat. We released the rest. We cast plugs but used diddly poles at night, catching catfish and turtles on them.

We passed Rodman, Iowa, the next day. Later in the afternoon, it started to rain. As we looked for a place to pitch the tent, it began to pour. We stopped, put up the tent, and got our supplies moved inside the shelter. We dried off the best we could and lay down, and went to sleep.

In the morning when we woke, only our heads and feet were out of the water! We hadn't picked a smart spot to pitch the tent. After we dried off and got everything loaded into the boat, we watched a large tree pass by. A good-sized boat happened to be chained to it. That's when we realized what a heavy rain it must have been.

The current was powerful that day. As we went fast around a bend, our boat ran onto a stump right in the middle of the river. We worked hard to balance on the stump and not tip the boat over. If it tipped, we would lose all our belongings in the current. We both worked up a pretty good sweat. After we tried to stay balanced for a while from the center of the boat, I crept to the back and used one oar to gradually push us off the stump. We slowed down as much as we could and made several stops that day.

We passed West Bend one day and weren't far from Bradgate another day. We needed to get ourselves to Rutland on the day and the hour when my dad planned to pick us up, but it was a challenge to figure out our location a lot of the time.

We never camped in a hollow again. It also didn't rain again on our trip, so we were lucky on that score. Only one farmer came down and told us we couldn't camp on his property. Our plugs snagged a lot while casting, but we never lost a plug or broke a line trying to get loose. We both lost a bit of weight because after the first couple of days, we only ate the fish and turtles we caught.

Rutland is located north of Humboldt and Fort Dodge. When we reached the dam, we carried our supplies, tent, and boat down below the dam, where we found a parking space. Both my mother and father showed up in a state-owned pickup truck shortly after we arrived. My mom had been worried about us! Max and I rode back to Spirit Lake in the back of the pickup truck, sitting in my boat.

Max ended up fighting in the Korean War. He returned home safe and went back to work for the State Conservation Commission.

....

ONE YEAR, TEAL DUCKS TOOK over one of the ponds my dad had helped dig for the state, the ones where they hatched walleye fingerlings to allow them to grow before placing them in area lakes. Hunting season began the first week in October.

On opening day of duck season, shooting wasn't allowed until noon. Hunters knew exactly when they were allowed to start because the Spirit Lake whistle always blew at noon.

Max snuck up on one side of the fingerling pond on opening day. An older bachelor whose big hunting dog always accompanied him snuck up from the opposite side. When the whistle blew, both hunters stood. The ducks flew up. The two hunters shot into the ducks before they flew very high. Max hit the older hunter in the butt with a lot of shot, which had to be removed by a doctor.

People laughed over that event for years in Orleans, Iowa.

Chapter 48

The Drake Relays

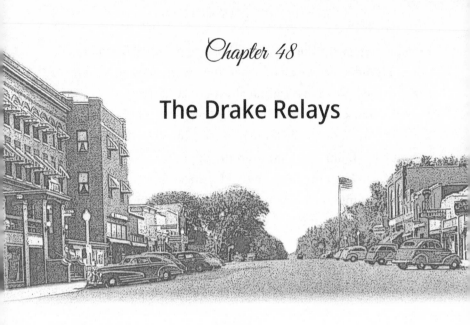

I FOUND OUT THAT HARRISON DILLARD was scheduled to run the high hurdles at the 1948 Drake Relays, the big collegiate meet for track teams back then. The relays were to be held on April 23 and 24. At the time, Harrison Dillard was the best hurdler in the world. He could run the 120-yard hurdles in fourteen seconds. I loved watching the high hurdles. I ran them a few times in high school but soon realized I was too short to be very good at the event.

We were high school seniors. For some reason, I couldn't drive my Model A. It must have been having mechanical issues at the time. So, I talked three other guys in my class into hitchhiking down to Des Moines with me: Harry Smith, Dave Dean, and Don Ahrens. Harry and Don were on our terrific two-mile relay team in track. Dave played football and basketball but didn't go out for track.

By car, the trip is 200 miles from Spirit Lake to Des Moines, Iowa. Drake University was on the east edge of Des Moines at the time, which is where the meet was held.

The four of us left after class on Friday. We decided to travel in groups of two so that we'd be more likely to get rides, and we'd have companionship. We were all fortunate to catch the rides we needed so that we all arrived in Des Moines before dark. We met at a large truck stop just north of the Drake campus. Not one of us brought very much money.

We walked to a business area and found an old hotel, where people who didn't have much money could stay. It cost either fifty cents or one dollar per night. The four of us went and ate something, returned to the old hotel, and each rented a bed. There were two long rows of single beds. We slept in adjacent beds and spent the night with our billfolds under our pillows.

In the morning, we ate a little breakfast and then walked out to the track. When we arrived, we discovered they charged a fee to get in. Dave Dean paid to enter and got his hand stamped with ink. He came back out, and all three of us held the back of our hand to his. Each of us transferred some of the ink stamp to our hands that way. We showed our inked hands at the entrance and were able to gain admission.

Because we were early to arrive, we were able to secure four seats next to the railing going around the track. We were right where the athletes would run the 100-yard dash directly in front of us. We were fortunate to be able to see the entire field—and all the events taking place in the middle—from our position on the west side of the track. The day was cold, and they ran the race from north to south. A big rugged-looking guy from Minnesota won, but it was a slow time.

When it came time for the high hurdles, the athletes all wore sweat suits, and they practiced with them on. They all took their sweat suits off when it was time to race, except for

Harrison Dillard. He left his top on. After he won the event, all the participants walked back to the starting point of the race. When he was right in front of us, we saw Harrison Dillard pull a fountain pen out from the top of his sweatshirt. He used the pen to sign autographs as he walked back to the starting point. I got a big kick out of that.

When we'd seen as much of the meet as we wanted, we walked back to the truck stop and ate some chips. We decided to travel two by two again, but while we were in the truck stop in line to use the restroom, Don Ahrens walked out to the highway and got a ride. After that, it seemed like we were all on our own. Harry Smith got a ride in an old Model A car. Then Dave Dean got a ride in a semi.

I got a short ride west on Highway 6 and 44 to Highway 4, which goes north. Then I got two or three rides going north on Highway 4. Around 9:00 p.m., I was let off at Emmetsburg. That's still forty miles from Spirit Lake, and darkness was falling. I walked to where the highway turned west and headed to Spencer. I was feeling pretty nervous about getting home.

A young guy stopped after ten minutes and picked me up. I told him I was headed to Spirit Lake. He said he had a date in Spencer and could take me that far, which was twenty miles. I assumed his girlfriend worked late, so they had to have a late date. When we got to the south end of Spencer, he said he had a little time and would take me to the hotel on the north end of Spencer that served as a bus stop.

That was better than my wildest dreams. His generosity really saved me because it was a long walk from the south end of Spencer to the north end. I got lucky when I ran into such a nice guy. Even though it was late, I was thrilled to find out there was still a bus going to Spirit Lake. What a relief! I arrived just a few minutes before the bus left. As soon as I sat down on the bench, the bus pulled in. It only cost a couple of dollars, and I had that much money. When I arrived at the Antler's Hotel in Spirit Lake, I called my dad. He came into town and picked me up.

Of the four of us, I had the most difficulty getting home that night. Harry had some trouble too. The farmer with the old Model A took Harry off the highway and left him at a crossroads that didn't have any traffic. He ended up hitching back to the highway to get another ride.

....

HARRISON DILLARD WAS THE TOP high hurdler in the world at the time of the 1948 Olympic trials. During the finals, Dillard hit a hurdle and fell, so he wasn't eligible to race in the Olympics. At the last minute, he decided to try out for the 100-yard dash.

The United States had who people thought were the two fastest sprinters in the world: Barney Ewell and Mel Patton. Harrison made the Olympic team as the third runner in the 100-yard dash. All three made it to the final race of the Olympics. The two American great runners were near the center of the track because they had the fastest times in the trial runs. Harrison was in the outside lane, the one usually reserved for the slowest qualifier. At the time, no one had ever won the 100-yard dash running in the outside lane. All eyes were on the men in the middle. Barney Ewell from the USA and Lloyd LaBeach from Panama placed second and third. Harrison Dillard, running in the outside lane, ended up winning the gold medal. I was so excited I couldn't speak.

For years afterward, a picture of Harrison Dillard winning that race hung in our garage. There wasn't anyone faster in those days. No wonder he'd won all those high-hurdle races. I picked him to be my hero, and he really lived up to it!

Harrison Dillard in the hurdles, 1948

....

DURING COLLEGE, I COMPETED IN the Drake Relays. Our mile relay team ran—we had a terrific mile relay team. When I was in high school, if someone could run the 440-yard dash in fifty seconds, they were really burning up the track. Our mile relay members all ran times of around forty-eight seconds. I could have pole vaulted, but I didn't want to make a fool of myself. I qualified, but all I had was a bamboo pole. In high school when I went to state, I used an aluminum pole which was even worse—it didn't bend at all. At least bamboo gave me a little push. With bamboo, I could lean back and go about one foot higher. The poles they use now seem like slingshots in comparison.

Chapter 49

Summer Employment

D URING THE SUMMER MONTHS, I worked for the Iowa
Conservation Commission. I worked with a rough
seining crew, trying to keep carp down in area lakes,
starting when I was twelve years old. After two years of seining,
I transferred to state construction projects and worked with
state dredge crews until I graduated from college. For the seining crew, our shifts were eight hours. But on construction and
dredging jobs, we worked twelve-hour days, six days a week.

We seined all around northwest Iowa. For a while, we were
at the north end of Big Spirit Lake. There's a great big bay,
and we seined carp up there. Seining game fish was not allowed. Only carp and other rough fish.

The state took bids on the seined carp, and most of them
went to Stoller Fisheries.

When we lived on the lake, I could go anywhere and catch
fish. Big Spirit Lake held plenty of walleye and other good-
tasting fish, so there was no reason for anyone who fished in
Spirit Lake to eat carp. Some of the old-timer bachelors liked

to smoke it though. They sometimes shared a couple of the carp with Dad, and then our family would eat that. Nobody else in the area liked to eat carp. Street vendors in Chicago bought it, though, and people there went crazy for it.

The first year I worked on the seining crew, the pay was $5.40 a day. My second year, it was $6.00 a day. The next year, it would have been $6.50, but I transferred to a construction crew because the pay was a dollar an hour. And since we worked twelve hours six days a week, I put in more hours per week and was able to earn more.

When I worked on construction projects for the Conservation Commission, we spent a lot of time dredging Five Island Lake near Emmetsburg. One of the workers owned a Ford station wagon with wood paneling on the exterior sides. He transported us to the site. A handful of us helped with dykes to hold the pumped-out mud. We worked on shore to move the pipeline that carried the mud too. We also shoveled or did whatever jobs the foreman gave us.

Later, I worked on Storm Lake. The Drinkies (a father and two sons) and I used to drive there a lot. The same dredge equipment was at Storm Lake for years. We actually used the same dredge years later on Silver Lake in Lake Park. That was the summer I met my future wife.

> A dredge is a large piece of equipment used to remove sediment from a lake or river.

Another guy and I cleared all the trees in an area on the east end of Storm Lake. We cut them down, chopped them up, and hauled them out so the town could put in a big park. There was a nightclub south of there with a dance hall and a restaurant, but we couldn't afford to eat there. I usually brought a sack lunch.

We also riprapped—dropping rocks along the shoreline to protect against water, ice, and wave erosion. We loaded the gravel trucks with rocks and drove to the bank along the lake. Then we backed up the trucks and dumped the rocks down along the lakeshore. However, it can be dangerous. If rocks get stuck in the tailgate, there's a danger the truck and driver could be thrown back into a somersault and down into the lake due to the weight of the load.

The summer before my junior year, I worked with the State of Iowa dynamite crew. We blew ditches between neighboring lakes. We waded through muddy sloughs all summer.

To deal with carp, we'd create a ditch between two adjacent lakes. I would dive down at the start of the ditch at one lake and plant dynamite with a cap. Then I'd set it off with an electrical plunger. That would create a large hole at that end of the lake. I did the same thing at the end of the ditch of the second lake.

The guys on the crew were all older and weren't involved in the swimming. At the lake that wasn't to be drained, we would build a dam at its entrance or exit. We'd drive down long metal sheets that fit together. One slid into the side of another. I operated a 110-pound air hammer with an end that fit over the metal sheet. I stood on a sheet that was driven down with the air hammer. One of the guys held on to my feet so I wouldn't fall off.

At the center of this dam, we built a slide opening so we could let the water run from the first lake (the smaller one) to the second lake, completely draining the lake to kill all the carp. If the carp returned, we could shut off the water and let the lake dry out again.

I set off almost all the dynamite chargers. The other guys were afraid to handle the blasting caps, and I didn't mind doing it. Most were family men, and I was too young to be concerned.

I'd put a cap in one of the dynamite sticks and run a line to a plunger to set off each blast. When we would pick up a box of blasting caps, I was designated to sit in the back of the pickup and hold on to them. The other guys were especially concerned if there was any lightning in the area. They claimed lightning could cause a cap to explode.

Sometimes with the explosions, a shower of rocks would fly over our heads. Once, we blew out the windows of two nearby farmhouses and had to pay for that.

Blasting with dynamite

Ditch created between two lakes

The Conservation Commission crew waiting for the next blast

One week, we were working to build a dyke for one of the dredges. First, we built a road out into the water. I backed up a load of dirt, dumped it, then got out of there. Then the next truck driver backed up and dumped, and so on. The temporary dirt road wasn't very solid, and one time I backed up, but the road gave way, and one of the axles broke. I was sixteen years old at the time.

Bob Boettcher from Spirit Lake drove to a nearby town to buy an axle. He worked for the Commission as an errand runner, buying parts or whatever was needed. He worked for Glen Powers, my sister Irene's second husband, who was head of the Conservation Commission. Our crew carried a huge toolbox with the tools needed, but the errand runner bought the axle.

All the other truckers stood around that day, and not one helped me. One wheel was working, one wasn't, and the axle was broken. I had to take the wheel off and remove the axle. I didn't know anything about changing an axle, but I had to take that axle out anyway.

Bob Boettcher, who later became the mayor of Spirit Lake, came back with the axle but was no help. He said he didn't know anything about axles either. He walked over to join the others.

I had to put that axle on and assemble everything together while those guys stood at a distance talking. Not one guy came over and helped me. I was sweating blood before I finished, but no one helped. I didn't ask either.

....

HARRY "SPEED" LYONS AND I worked at this same lake another time, down in the middle of Iowa. While I dumped one load of dirt, he had care of the other two trucks. He got one filled and then started on the other. I ran back as fast as I could, parked the just-emptied truck, and took a full one. We worked like that the entire day.

The Commission had a limitless supply of rocks for any construction project. My dad had that giant rock pile on the hill behind his house—the ones from the farm fields. Likewise, many farmers had big piles of rocks they were happy to get rid of. Speed would load the dragline onto a flatbed, and we'd pick up a truckload of rocks from whatever farmer he'd made plans with. At the site, he'd use the dragline again to drop them along the shoreline.

When it was just the two of us working, I dropped dirt over the rocks once they were in place. I'd run and jump in the truck, drive the load over, come back, and get the next load. That was hard work. It's a good thing I was young and didn't know any better.

....

BRITT, IOWA, WAS A LITTLE town near one of the lakes where we worked. Once a year, they hosted Hobo Day. The whole town celebrated. Hobos came from all over the country. Since it was Hobo Day, everything was free for them. The town elected a winner and called him "King of the Hobos."

> Hobos were migratory workers who helped meet America's labor needs starting after the Civil War. Homeless by choice, they "worked to travel and traveled to work," mostly moving around by freight trains.[8]

---

8. Britt Hobo Days (website), retrieved May 26, 2023, https://www.brittho-bodays.com.

Speed and I went to see Hobo Day once. There were carnival rides and games with barkers calling out to attract patrons. People came in from all the nearby towns to attend the celebration.

The town filled the square with tents, and people called out, "Come and see the two-headed woman," and so on. The event was spread all over town. It was really a big deal.

....

DURING MY HIGH SCHOOL SUMMERS, I sometimes worked as a guide for Grandpa. If his two guides were out with fishing parties and a couple of fishermen came in to rent a boat and wanted a guide, I'd help out.

I worked for the state twelve hours a day the rest of the week, but I'd help Grandpa on Sundays.

Customers could rent a boat from the livery for three dollars a day. A motor cost five dollars. Hiring me as a guide cost six dollars per day. I don't know what the other guides made, but they earned at least six dollars plus a bonus. In addition, the customers would take the guide out for lunch at noon. Because I was a kid, no one ever bought my lunch. I had to do everything the full-time guides did, but I only made six dollars. Including the bonus, the guides probably earned ten dollars plus their lunch.

Those were big boats—sixteen feet long and really heavy. It was hard work for one person to pull them up on the shore. Often there was a motor on the back in addition to two guys, the tackle, and everything else.

If I wasn't needed as a guide for Grandpa, I'd go wash cars all day at the gas station. My brother-in-law Jerry ran the Mobil station on the west side of the road for a while. The two brothers who ran the Standard station were getting up in age, so Jerry left the Mobil and rented the Standard station. He hired a good mechanic and brought in a lot of service work. For rent, he paid the brothers five cents for every gallon of gas he sold. He offered car washes, but the mechanic refused to wash cars, so I helped Jerry out when I could.

After two years, he started selling new Nash Ambassador automobiles. Near one end of the gas station, he always displayed a large For Sale sign and a couple of Nash Ambassadors.

Summer Work Record			
Year	Age/Grade	Job	Earnings
1941	Age 11, after 5th Grade	Worked at Egralharve all summer	$1.00 (plus lawn work earnings)
1942	Age 12	Worked on seining crew as an extra worker	$5.40/ day for an 8-hour workday
1943	Age 13	Worked on carp seining crew—they had a small crew that worked all year also.	$6.00/day for an 8-hour workday
1943	Age 13	Quit working the seining crew one week early to work on threshing crew shoveling oats into bins.	$1.00/hour
1944	Age 14	Started working on state construction crew. Worked short jobs for two different dredges: Storm Lake and Emmetsburg (5 Mile Lake)	$1.00/hour
1945	Age 15	Kept working on state crew with foreman as boss. Took down old sea wall at Arnold's Park with an electric drill. Built new cement wall with wheelbarrows full of cement	$1.00/hour (plus misc. jobs)
1946	Age 16	Worked with four-man regular crew of dump truck drivers all over state of Iowa. I drove the 5th dump truck, built a dirt wall for one of the dredges, dumped large rocks and dirt on shoreline to stop erosion. (Speed Lyons with drag line with us)	$1.40/hour
1947	Age 17	Worked with dynamite crew all summer. Blew a ditch between two lakes. Blasted a hole at start of each lake. Built a dam at upper lake to control flow to lower lake. Built electric fence to keep cattle from lake.	$1.40/hour
1948	Age 18, after 12th grade	Worked on drag line with Speed Lyons. Built dirt walls for dredges. Miscellaneous jobs around lakes	$1.40/hour
1948-1952	Ages 18-22	Worked on dredge every summer at Lake Park. Plus two of us cut down the trees on the east end of Storm Lake for a park to be built. We hauled all the wood away. We used axes and a two-man saw.	$1.70/hour

Chapter 50

The Longest Day

GRANDPA'S BROTHER JOE ASKED ME if I would help seine carp up at Heron Lake in Minnesota. I said I was available since the job would be on a Sunday. This was during the summers when I worked the other six days of the week, twelve hours a day, on a construction crew for the State of Iowa. At the time, I was sixteen or seventeen.

I figured out later that Joe wanted my help with his scheme because I had two years of experience working on the seining crew. None of the other guys were experienced.

The laws had changed, and commercial seining was no longer allowed in Iowa lakes. Seining was still permitted in the Mississippi River, but only state crews were allowed to seine rough fish such as carp, buffalo, and sheepshead in lakes. Commercial seining was still legal across the border in Minnesota though.

I arrived at the Burr Oak Livery at four o'clock on Sunday morning. My great-uncle Joe owned the livery, but his brother Levi managed the business. The man who worked for Levi at the boathouse had a semi-full of fish boxes and a seine ready to go when I arrived. We drove up to South Heron Lake. I learned that morning that there were actually two Heron Lakes—Heron and South Heron. In addition, a slough off South Heron Lake held carp too.

An older guy with only one eye came out to meet us. He lived in a small house close to the slough and the lake. Joe had hired him as a guide to tell us where to seine. The man had trapped plenty of carp in between the lake and the slough. He ate some of the carp but sold most of them. He knew where the carp could be found.

Two or three carloads arrived with guys to help us seine. Levi's boathouse employee was supposed to lead the work, but he needed me to tell him how to seine since he had never done it before.

We got the seine out and began to work. The one-eyed man pointed to an area, and we seined it. We threw the carp into the wooden boxes. The boxes had a wooden handle on each end. While some of us seined the next area, two guys carried the box of fish up the hill to the semi-trailer. We took occasional breaks to walk to the truck and move the boxes of fish to the front of the trailer, stacking them up.

At noon, Joe pulled up in a big car to check how we were doing. He brought a case of beer and sandwiches with him. We all sat and ate a sandwich and drank a cold beer while Levi's employee explained our progress to Joe. Joe drove off, and we continued to seine haul after haul, filling the semi with fish. Darkness fell, and we were still seining carp. Joe must have given the Burr Oak employee information on how many boxes were needed for the order. We kept working until the boxes were filled.

When we arrived back at the livery, we had been gone twenty hours. That is my record for the number of hours I worked in one day. None of the guys talked about the wages they earned, and I can't remember how much Joe ended up paying me. It was probably about a dollar an hour or a little more.

I have no idea where he borrowed or rented the seine, the wooden boxes, or the semi-truck, but it became clear to me that Joe put a lot of effort into planning that day.

After we returned with the load, Joe still needed all the fish gutted and packed on ice to get them shipped quickly. I went home and fell into bed, and never asked or heard about those details.

Chapter 51

Time with Friends

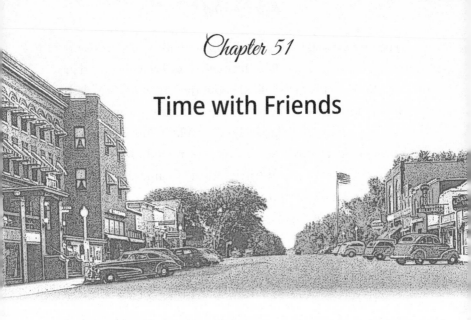

DUD (HARRY) SMITH NEVER HAD a car when he was in high school. Neither did Dave Dean or Don Ahrens. Tom Carver drove a convertible for a while until his dad sold it. Later, he drove an old Model T for a year or so.

Most of my friends didn't have a car. If they wanted to go to Arnolds Park, we'd ride in my coupe. Since only a couple of guys could fit into my car, if more wanted to go, I'd borrow Dad's big red Buick. We'd drive down to the roller rink, stand outside, listen to the organ music, and watch people.

Nobody ever offered to help pay for gas. I always bought my own gas, and when I borrowed Dad's car, I had to replace the fuel we used. I was a serious penny pincher, but my friends were as bad or worse. None of us ever had much money. We could never go on any of the rides at Arnolds Park. Well, I could have. I had money, but I wasn't going to spend it. As soon as I started earning money at the age of eight, I tried to save every nickel I could for college. I bought my own clothes after sixth grade, but that was about it. I never dated much either.

Tommy Carver

Harry Dudley Smith

Jim Norman

Don Ahrens

Dave Dean

....

BOB WAUGH WAS A NICE guy, a year younger than me. I knew
him from track and would help him run the 880-relay sometimes. The relay was his only event. Occasionally, if we were
competing in a small meet or if we were going to win anyway,
I would tell the coach I was too busy in the middle of the track
with the high jump and the pole vault. When I told the coach
I didn't think I could make it over for the relay, he'd let Bob
run in my place.

Bob invited me to his house a couple of times. His dad,
Hubie (Hubert), had one glass eye. I never asked how he lost
his eye. My buddy Jim Norman's brother (Stan Norman) had
a glass eye too. Stan was a few years older than us. He and two
other guys were walking along a road, and a car kicked up a
rock that put out his eye.

Bob Waugh was dating a girl in Estherville who planned
to be a nurse. The girl had a friend, so Bob wanted me to go
along one time, and I agreed. He borrowed his dad's car that
night.

When we arrived, it turned out the other girl was my cousin. My mom had eleven brothers and sisters. I hadn't met some
of my cousins, but I knew their names and where they lived.

The folks often talked about the Georges who lived near
Estherville. I knew that Viola George was one of my mom's
older sisters. Bob's date's friend was a nice-looking, dark-haired
girl. But when I met her and heard her name, it dawned on me
that the George girl was probably my cousin.

Once I heard her name that night, I didn't sit close to her
or hold her hand or anything. Bob and his girlfriend were busy
kissing in one corner. I pretty much hung out over in another
corner of the rec room by myself. The poor George girl must

have been very disappointed in her date. I was too embarrassed to say anything to her about being cousins, and I don't think she knew.

Neil Nelson, Spirit Lake HS graduation photo

Chapter 52

College Room
and Board

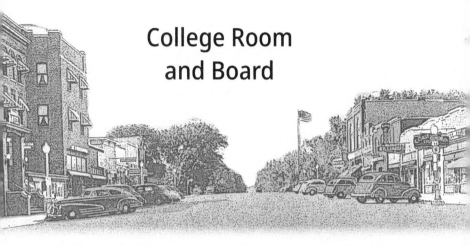

T OMMY CARVER WAS MY GREATEST friend, but I didn't
realize it until much later in life. We started kindergarten together and were classmates all through our
school days. It's a shame that we can have close friends all
through our school years, but after graduation everyone scat-
ters and loses contact.

Tommy is the one who talked me into going to the
University of South Dakota in Vermillion. His older brother
Bill had attended the university and found work afterward in
Sioux Falls. Tommy's other older brother Glen wasn't inter-
ested in college. He worked at the Maytag store with his dad.

After Tommy talked me into South Dakota, I drove there
and found out that tuition cost 50 percent more for out-of-
state students than for residents. Even so, South Dakota was
inexpensive compared with other universities.

Tuition cost forty dollars a semester for residents and sixty
dollars for out-of-state students. Also, out-of-state students

needed to maintain a standing in the top third or fourth of their class.

The second time I drove home from Vermillion, my car broke down. A piston had broken. I didn't think it was fixable on the old Model A, so I sold my car to the dump for twenty-five dollars. Dad put a chain on it and helped me get it there.

During my first two years of college, I didn't have a car. None of my friends did either.

I hitchhiked home most weekends. I missed my parents, and I wanted to eat my mom's cooking. I could study in Spirit Lake comfortably and eat good food for free. If I could have found someone with a car who was headed in the direction of home on the weekends, that would have been nice. Twice, I got a ride with a guy who lived between Spencer and Hartley. Then all I had to do was hitchhike from there.

Tommy must have sold his Model T when he went to college because he never had a car there. Harry Smith came to South Dakota during my last year, but he didn't have a car either.

Tommy joined the Alpha Tau Omega (ATO) fraternity because his brother had belonged. After he talked to me the whole semester about it, I joined for the second semester. The upstairs of the house had bunk beds. We lived there and were provided one or two meals a day. A woman ran the place, cooked, and cleaned. The price wasn't too high, and I ate better that semester than the rest of my college years. But too many of those guys wanted to party, and I didn't have extra money for that. And I didn't enjoy being a pledge. The older boys ordered us around, and I didn't care for that, so I only stayed one semester.

The university didn't have dorms for men, only for women. I bunked for a while at the student union, and then I rented a room from an older woman. I boarded with her for quite a while.

The landlady, Mrs. Mounts, had really strict rules. The room contained a bed and a desk where I could study. The bathroom was down the hall. I was allowed one light bulb in the middle of the room. She did not permit more than a 40-watt light bulb, and I had to be careful to turn off the light whenever I left.

Tommy had also talked our classmate Jim Norman into coming to South Dakota. Jim, Tommy, and I roomed together for a while at Mrs. Mounts' place. She lived in the downstairs of her home and rented rooms upstairs. The three of us shared a bathroom upstairs. Mrs. Mounts also wall-papered residences to earn a living. She had a funny way of sighing as she talked, so we imitated her a lot, but she was a nice person.

Before long, Jim Norman joined a different fraternity. He'd planned to go out for basketball but never did. It was the same thing for Tommy Carver. He had been our track captain, and he'd planned to go out for track, but he never did. I'm the only one who got involved with a sport when I walked out for the track team and made it.

Jim left school and joined the Air Force. He ended up marrying a girl from Lorenz, Iowa. He wrote to me while he served in the Air Force that they were married. Jim later opened a Ford dealership in Primghar, Iowa, and ran that for more than forty years.

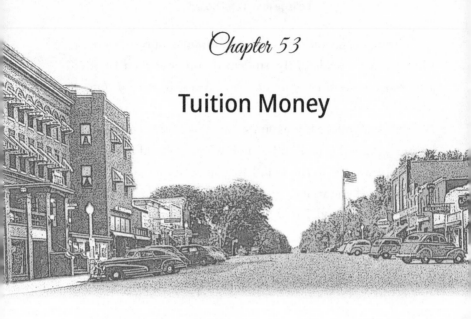

Chapter 53

Tuition Money

HARRY (DUD) SMITH, AL EICHINGER, and I rented a basement apartment with beds and a kitchen during my fifth and final year at South Dakota. The bathroom and shower were down the hall. The place was convenient—right next door to the school.

I was working on a double major in engineering and business. Al Eichinger studied law, and Harry took basic, first-year courses. He planned to study accounting.

Though it was my last year, it was Dud's first year because of his time in the service.

He joined the Army right after high school. After two years, his enlistment was up, and he was discharged while in Japan. But the Korean War started, and Harry got called right back in—they sent him right back to Japan. And from Japan to Korea.

The poor guy saw a lot of action. A terrible amount. He and his squad were walking behind a tank when it hit one or two land mines, and the whole squad was killed except Dud. In one moment, his eight buddies were all gone. After that, the Army appointed him squad leader, and he was assigned eight young kids for his new squad.

When Harry left Korea, he came and joined me at the University of South Dakota. He could only afford to attend college because of the G.I. Bill.

Another law student friend of ours stayed in the same room I had previously rented with the landlady who only allowed the single 40-watt light bulb. He often played pranks on people. Radio stations used to have giveaways. He would call and tell friends they had won money and to come down to the radio station to pick it up. He was always doing stuff like that.

One weekend, I went home and brought back a big old carp. Dud and I wrapped it in newspapers, snuck into his room, and stuck it between his mattresses. The landlady complained about the smell, and our friend got pretty worked up about it. Harry and I snuck back into his room while he was in class. We took the fish out, and we never did tell him. We should have, but we didn't.

As I approached my last semester of college, I was out of money. Most of my life, I had worked and saved for college, and now I had absolutely no idea where I'd get the funds for my final tuition payment. Harry had the G.I. Bill, so his room and board were covered. He could go to a designated place for all his meals, and they were paid for.

For breakfast each day, I ate a donut with coffee. For lunch, I ordered a hamburger and coffee. I didn't eat much because I didn't have much money. In the basement, I could fix pancakes for supper.

Harry wanted to go see a certain movie. I'd seen the movie and didn't want to spend money to see it again. I hated seeing movies twice. I finally gave in to his pestering and went with him. The movie was on Wednesday, and the theater had a drawing each Thursday night. Those in attendance on Wednesday could sign a slip and put it in a box.

A couple of days later, I got a phone call to come down to the theater. "You've won money," the girl said.

I told Dud that I knew our law student friend was playing a prank. I didn't think much about it. Still, on Monday, I gave in and went down to the theater, just in case. They handed me 450 dollars in fifty-dollar bills.

I now had money to pay my tuition costs for my final semester. A big weight had fallen off my shoulders. I bought my dad a radio for his pickup truck. It cost fifty dollars. And I bought DorEtta, my girlfriend and future wife, a turntable that she never liked. I found out years later it was because she had been hoping for an engagement ring.

I've always believed winning that movie drawing saved my life in a way. If I hadn't won that cash, I wouldn't have graduated.

....

TOMMY CARVER MARRIED A WOMAN who worked as a teacher. I don't know if he ever got into photography or what he did for work. I should have kept better track of him, but we were each busy with our own lives and our new marriages. And my company kept moving me from place to place.

I did learn that Tommy and his wife had one child. They'd lived behind his folks' house in an apartment above their garage. Tommy discovered some sort of problem with his leg, and a doctor in Rochester told him it was cancer. He lived less than a year after the diagnosis. Tommy passed away in 1956 at the age of twenty-seven, leaving behind his wife and their little child.

After I graduated, Harry Smith transferred from the University of South Dakota to Iowa University. He later moved to Los Angeles. Another Spirit Lake classmate who attended Iowa University with Harry called my wife and me a few times over the years. She kept track of Harry for a while. According to her, he was doing well. He worked for a large business, made a good living, and even came up with a particularly innovative idea for the company.

Harry had worked as a golf caddy as a kid, and he kept up with golfing. After he retired, he moved to Arizona. He even ran his own golf tournament there. I was proud of him. He turned out pretty great.

During my college years, I lived at home each summer so I could work and earn money for more college. I worked on the dredge in Lake Park every summer. Speed Lyons and I sometimes ate lunch in a restaurant on the main street in town. DorEtta Petersen worked there as a waitress. That's how we met.

We dated for a couple of years and married right after my college graduation. After graduation, I headed to officer training in Tacoma, Washington. The Korean conflict ended around that time, and I was released from training.

I worked as a manufacturing engineer for J.I. Case. They moved us around from Rockford, Illinois, to Davenport, Iowa, to Clinton, Iowa, to Racine, Wisconsin, and even to Anniston, Alabama. In fact, DorEtta and I moved eighteen times in our first two years of marriage. That made it tough for friends to keep current with our address and phone number.

We raised our three children in northern Illinois and southern Wisconsin. After some years with J.I. Case, I was employed by Western Newell (now called Newell Operating Company). Later I worked for A. O. Smith Harvestore.

DorEtta and I visited our family in northwest Iowa at least once or twice each year. We talked several times about moving back someday. After we retired, we once again considered returning to our Iowan roots. We even house-hunted a little, but in our sixty-five years of marriage, we never did move back.

They say you can't go home—that things will never be the same. Maybe that's true. But I'm grateful for the memories I have of my growing-up years. I'm thankful for the good remembrances I have of time spent with my folks, my grandparents, my sisters, relatives, neighbors, and friends.

I'll always have fond memories of Spirit Lake and trips to town.

(left) Mom's L-shaped restaurant; (right) The folks' cottage on Big Spirit Lake

University of South Dakota graduation photo

Wedding day photo of DorEtta and Neil

Four generations of Nelsons: (from left) Grandpa Dave Nelson, Neil's young namesake, Neil D. Nelson, Neil's dad (Neil Swailes Nelson)

SPIRIT LAKE

Acknowledgments

OKOBOJI LAKE

M Y DEEP APPRECIATION GOES TO Michelle Rayburn for her editing, cover design, and typesetting.

I am indebted to my writer friends Robin Steinweg, Joanie Shawhan, and Anita Klumpers. Their encouragement, edits, and suggestions have been invaluable.

I appreciate the kind assistance of Julie Belanger of Descendants of WWII Rangers, Inc. when I reached out regarding Ranger photos. And my gratitude goes to the librarians at Sun Prairie Public Library for their friendly service.

For generously sharing family photos, thank you to Bob and Sharon Kelley.

Finally, thank you to my husband, Mark, and my daughters, Paige and Sally, for the many ways they helped me with this project.

Made in the USA
Las Vegas, NV
23 June 2024

91368765R00125